W9-BJT-581

✧ ✧ ✧ ✧ ✧ ✧ ✧ ✧ ✧ ✧ ✧

Healing and Transformation in Sandplay

❖ ❖ ❖ ❖ ❖ ❖ ❖ ❖ ❖ ❖

Healing and Transformation in Sandplay
Creative Processes Made Visible

Ruth Ammann

Translated by Wolf-Dieter Peter Rainer

Foreword by Donald Sandner

OPEN COURT
Chicago and La Salle, Illinois

To order books from Open Court, call toll-free 1-800-815-2280.
This book has been reproduced in a print-on-demand format from the 1991 Open Court printing.

THE REALITY OF THE PSYCHE SERIES

Open Court Publishing Company is a division of
Carus Publishing Company.

©1991 by Open Court Publishing Company

First printing 1991

All rights reserved. No part of this publication may be
reproduced, stored in a retrieval system, or transmitted, in any
form or by any means, electronic, mechanical, photocopying,
recording, or otherwise, without the prior written permission of
the publisher, Open Court Publishing Company, La Salle,
Illinois 61301.

Printed and bound in the United States of America.

Library of Congress Cataloging-in-Publication Data

Ammann, Ruth, 1934–
    [Heilende Bilder der Seele. English]
    Healing and transformation in sandplay : creative processes
made visible / Ruth Ammann ; translated by Wolf-Dieter Peter
Rainer ; foreword by Donald Sandner.
       p.   cm. — (The Reality of the psyche series)
    Translation of: Heilende Bilder der Seele.
    Includes bibliographical references and index.
    ISBN 0–8126–9140–7. — ISBN 0–8126–9141–5 (pbk.)
    1. Sandplay—Therapeutic use—Case studies. I. Title.
II. Title: Healing and transformation in sand play. III. Series.
RC489.S25A4413   1991
616.89'17—dc20   91–18685
                                                 CIP

❖ ❖ ❖ ❖ ❖ ❖ ❖ ❖ ❖ ❖ ❖

For my mother
and for my father

Contents

✧ ✧ ✧ ✧ ✧ ✧ ✧ ✧ ✧ ✧ ✧

Illustrations

NOTE: Illustrations 16–47, which are vital for understanding the three case-histories, also appear in full color between pages 74 and 75.

Foreword

In 1916, near the end of his turbulent period of inner development, Jung wrote an important paper called 'The Transcendent Function', but he did not release it for publication until nearly 40 years later. Possibly he was reluctant to present this paper to the professional world because it represented a departure from the usual analytic technique. It did, in fact, represent something that could hardly be called 'analysis' at all. He said: "An emotional disturbance can also be dealt with in another way, not by clarifying it intellectually but by giving it visible shape. Patients who possess some talent for drawing or painting can give expression to their mood by means of a picture. It is not important for the picture to be technically or aesthetically satisfying, but merely for the fantasy to have free play and for the whole thing to be done as well as possible." (Vol. 8, CW, pp. 82–83) Besides giving unconscious contents visual shape, Jung also mentioned conversing with inner voices and moving (or dancing) in response to inner dictates.

Although Jung did not speak of it specifically, we may include sandplay here also. Each of these various modalities has its own special relevance to the individual patient. Some patients have a talent for drawing or modelling clay, others are greatly introverted and have always heard voices in their psyches. But almost everyone has a history in childhood of playing in the sand, building sandcastles at the beach or constructing whole scenes in a back yard sand box. Indeed, my son, who was four or five at the time I got my first sand tray, said when he first saw it: "That's too small! They'll never be able to get inside." Maybe he was right. Maybe a greater experience would be to have a big sand box and climb right inside, but, alas, as adults (and adults dealing with children) we can allow only a smaller symbolic sandplay space. But we make up for that with a magnificent array of imaginative figurines, all to·be used in the sand tray, or discarded, as the patient sees fit. The kingdom of childhood is opened once more by sandplay, and with it the door to the deep unconscious and its mysteries.

Even though the techniques of sand tray psychology are relatively young, the act of visioning (which is the central activity here) is not. It goes back to the earliest dawn of human consciousness and the first shamans were there to perform it. Their visions were a mainstay of the tribe, a means to heal and to invoke good fortune. The eyes of visioning could find a way where other eyes were blind. Then came the civilized era with its prophets, mystics, and mediums, putting their ability to envision at the service of the established religion. Finally in Jung's psychology, especially in active imagination, including the sand tray, there is another path for this ancient art.

The vision—as differentiated from the dream—allows us to consciously peer into the psyche and record in some form the symbolic images we see there. As always, the meaning of these images cannot be fully understood by the intellect, but it can be experienced and known by the psyche as a whole.

This visioning process, besides presenting symbolic images to the conscious mind, enlarges an area of the psyche which can be used to contain these images, to reflect on them, to allow them to interact with one another, or to enter into creative sandplay. All this is active imagination, and once it has been nurtured it becomes another dimension of the mind. Henry Corbin called this the *mundus imaginalis*. He said: "there is a world that is both intermediary and immediate . . . the world of the image, the *mundus imaginalis*: a world that is ontologically as real as the world of the senses and that of the intellect. This world requires its own faculty of perception, namely, imaginative power, a faculty with a cognitive function, a noetic value which is as real as that of sense perception or intellectual intention." It is this ancient faculty which is put to use again in the sand tray.

Even the use of sand itself to record inner visions has a long history. Many Native Americans, especially the Navaho and the Hopi in the Southwest, and the Dieaueño and Luiseño in Southern California, made extensive use of sand paintings in their healing and initiation ceremonies. With the Navaho the use of paintings in sand was the main feature of a vast healing system which surrounded the patient with all the powerful symbolism of the Navaho mythic world creating the conditions for a restoration of harmony and wellbeing. The sand paintings themselves were traditional figures: animals, plants, natural forms such as winds, storms, rain, hail, gods and goddesses—all of which had a place in the Navaho cosmos, and were a kind of legacy from the shamanic era during which the ancestors of the Navaho wandered in slow migration down from Alaska to the present-day Southwest. During that time they originated a remarkable healing religion by embodying their original shamanic visions in sand. Then for each healing ceremony, for each patient, the ancient visions were reproduced again in sand pictures, filled with original power, and used by the medicine man to conduct this power into the patient as he sat on the painting. In this way American Indians have a very intimate connection with the recording and use of visions in sand, and I have heard it reported that they are amenable to this kind of imaginative psychological work because it uses their own traditional medium.

But however old and universal the art of visioning, and even its incorporation in sand, each era has its own techniques and perspectives for it. Our modern viewpoint, more personal, more psychological, more flexible than the old ways, is presented in this book by Ruth Ammann (admirably translated from the German by Wolf-Dieter Peter Rainer) with a verve, imaginative play and depth of psychological understanding that breathes a new life into the old methods. Developed from the lifelong labor and dedication of Dora Kalff, this method is here explained and expanded by the continued and equally dedicated efforts of Ruth Ammann. Here the technique and philosophy of sand tray work is given definitive form and with this book, more than any others I have seen, sand tray psychology comes of age.

Particularly significant are the presentations in sand pictures and accompanying texts of major segments in the work of three analytic patients. These case studies comprise a full and complete description of the sand tray healing process. They are worth careful study.

The first is that of Eva, a severely depressed middle-aged woman, in which the symbolism of death and rebirth, the heart of any deep healing experiences, is revealed in 16 sandplay pictures wih lucid explanations. These are very personal and moving statements of Eva's struggle, but they also bear unmistakable elements of archetypal structure of the kind that is found also in traditional tribal sand paintings. We find the central mountain as world axis (Eva's sand pictures 6, 15, and 16); the world divided into four quarters (sand picture 1); the round dance (sand picture 5); a complex mandala (sand picture 16); and the snake meander and spiral (sand picture 10) among the most obvious ones. Interestingly, Eva's sand picture number 2, which is entirely made up of an image drawn in the sand of the face of the sun, is very similar in spirit, if different in style, to the Navaho sand painting also of the face of Sun made as part of Hail Way. In this great healing ritual the patient sits on the sand painting of the Sun and absorbs the power of that great natural force, which is that of a god. Ruth Ammann says of Eva's painting that it radiates "power and effect from within, our personal sun as archetype, as it were, can be felt." Sometimes the personal touches the archetype in a striking way.

The second case study is that of a seven-year-old child, Maria. Her pictures include great numbers of animals and demonstrate movements of energy within the psyche that are carefully and lovingly described in the text. These pictures in themselves could be seen as symbols of childhood development, and are very different from any traditional sand paintings. The order and symmetry of the adult's inner psyche has not been achieved, but the great sprawling, surging, intense emotionality of the child is laid out before us. We can see in three dimensions the great flow of energy free itself from developmental trauma and stream toward the future.

The last case study of Elizabeth, a 40-year-old married woman who wanted to prepare herself for a professional career, is perhaps the most conscious and differentiated one. It displays the course of feminine development in a highly individualized way in which the sand figures almost come to represent in themselves the complexes and archetypal determinants of her psyche.

With this book and these beautifully presented cases, the new technique of sandplay therapy reaches an effectiveness that should make it attractive to a wide range of psychotherapists, especially those interested in the visionary aspects of the psyche. As Jung said at the very end of his long unpublished manuscript 'The Transcendent Function': "It is a way of obtaining liberation by one's own efforts and of finding the courage to be oneself." (CW 8, p. 193)

Donald Sandner

Preface

Sandplay is a method of psychotherapy based on practical, creative work in the sand tray. Whether adult or child, the person at the sand tray, the person creating various three-dimensional pictures in the sand, is involved with body, soul, and spirit in this process.

Thank to the 'hands-on' method of sandplay, both the spiritual and psychological dimensions are not merely constellated in the person, but they are, at the same time, given physical form by the person's hands. For this reason, persons who are blocked psychologically or out of touch with their imaginative powers often find this aspect of sandplay to be particularly therapeutic. Working with their hands at the sand tray mobilizes these creative energies and gets them flowing again.

The therapeutic method of sandplay was developed by Dora M. Kalff from Margareth Lowenfeldt's 'World Technique', as for example Charlotte Buhler's 'World Test' or the so-called 'Erica Method' which has been used in Sweden for over 40 years as a diagnostic tool in child psychiatry.[1] Dora Kalff recognized that a series of sand pictures created by either children or adults actually represents a continuing practical confrontation with the unconscious and is comparable to a series of dreams or to active imagination occurring during the analytic process. It is clear that working at the sand tray initiates a psychic process which is holistic and can lead to healing and the development of the personality.[2]

I have been extraordinarily impressed by this method since it can provide the grounds for the interaction of body and psyche, matter and spirit. Sandplay creates a common field within which spirit and body can mutually influence each other. Such direct interplay between psyche and matter is not known, at least in this form, in classical verbal analysis.

It is for this reason that I believe that classical dream analysis and sandplay belong together. They represent two equally valid therapeutic approaches which allow us to adapt better to the psychological needs of the analysand. Both methods are founded on the psychology of C.G. Jung. Dora Kalff herself based sandplay on his psychology. In his chapter on 'Confrontation with the Unconscious' in *Memories, Dreams, Reflections,* Jung writes of his own experience with sandplay:

The dreams, however, could not help me over my feeling of disorientation. On the contrary, I lived as if under constant inner pressure. At times this became so strong that I suspected there was some psychic disturbance in myself. Therefore I twice went over all the details of my entire life, with particular attention to childhood memories; for I thought there might be something in my past which I could not see and which might possibly be the cause of the disturbance. But this retrospection led to nothing but a fresh acknowledgment of my own ignorance. Thereupon I said to myself, "Since I know nothing at all, I shall simply do whatever occurs to me." Thus I *consciously submitted myself to the impulses of the unconscious.*

The first thing that came to the surface was a childhood memory from perhaps my tenth or eleventh year. At that time I had a spell of playing passionately with building blocks. I distinctly recalled how I had built little houses and castles, using bottles to form the sides of gates and vaults. Somewhat later I had used ordinary stones, with mud for mortar. These structures had fascinated me for a long time. To my astonishment, this memory was accompanied by a good deal of emotion. "Aha," I said to myself, "there is still life in these things. The small boy is still around, and posesses a *creative life* which I lack. But how can I make my way to it?" For as a grown man it seemed impossible to me that I should be able to bridge the distance from the present back to my eleventh year. Yet if I wanted to re-establish contact with that period, I had no choice but to return to it and take up once more that child's life with his childish games. This moment was a turning point in my fate, but I gave in only after endless resistances and with a sense of resignation. For it was a painfully humiliating experience to realize that there was nothing to be done except play childish games . . .

I went on with my building game after the noon meal every day, whenever the weather permitted. As soon as I was through eating, I began playing, and continued to do so until the patients arrived; and if I was finished with my work early enough in the evening, I went back to building. *In the course of this activity my thought clarified, and I was able to grasp the fantasies whose presence in myself I dimly felt.*

Naturally, I thought about the significance of what I was doing, and asked myself, "Now, really, what are you about? You are building a small town, and doing it as if it were a rite!" I had no answer to my question, only the inner certainty that I was *on the way to discovering my own myth.* For the building game was only a beginning. It released a stream of fantasies which I later carefully wrote down.

This sort of thing has been consistent with me, and at any time in my later life when I came up against a blank wall, I painted a picture or hewed stone. Each such experience proved to be a *rite d'entree* for the ideas and works that followed hard upon it.[3] [emphasis added]

It is my view that we should increasingly include the body and the non-rational, imaginal world within psychotherapy because these dimensions are gaining in importance and they must, indeed, continue to do so. While the value of logical thinking has been stressed for a long time, these other values have been denied their importance. Jungian analysts are well aware of this view but more often than not, it is not sufficiently applied in practice.

There is another reason why we need a therapeutic complement to our current analytical practice. In our offices we see more and more clients who clearly suffer from disturbances of a narcissistic nature or disturbances rooted in early childhood. Often these are referred to as disturbances of the primal relationship, or Urbeziehung, to use Neumann's original word. Many such disturbances may have been caused by the overemphasis of the rational side (with its attendant focus on achievement) during our school years and career development. As a corollary, our feeling life, along with our natural, instinctual drives have received little support or may even have atrophied. These phenomena can be seen today especially among mothers, many of whom have great difficulty in loving their child while it is still in the womb and later when it is growing up. Today many a mother has lost the ability to devote herself to her children so that they might experience an inner relationship and loving way with her. The child is not given the loving warmth and security so necessary during the first few years of life.[4]

And yet, I do not wish here to single out and accuse mothers and fathers, for they themselves might live in insecurity and without love, living in a society, as we do, which neglects compassion and the development of a community of shared values.

Sandplay, then, is especially suited for those adults and children who suffer from disturbances of early childhood because sandplay can—nonverbally—lead the person back into the deeper layers of the early childhood psyche.

During my analytical work I use both verbal analysis and sandplay simultaneously. But it can happen that an analysand first expresses himself through sandplay and then, later, after working through the sand pictures analytically, continues with dream analysis. Another possibility is that an analysand alternates between a verbal analysis and sandplay. He may perhaps create especially important stations of his process in a sand picture or treat specific or especially difficult themes or transitions in the sand.

I was attracted to the sandplay method from the moment I first encountered it. One reason for this attraction lies surely in my love of images and three-dimensional forms. This has always been close to my heart, especially since I like to use my hands. Another reason for my preference may lie in the fact that I experienced early in life the way in which one can use one's senses in a differentiated way without words. As a young child I observed my grandfather in his medical practice behave in just this way. For instance, I was deeply struck by the following experience. My grandfather, who was a pediatrician, had also set up a room for consultations in his home and would occasionally see patients there. As a small girl I once observed through the keyhole how he examined an infant. He inspected the child from all sides, touching, listening, and probing everywhere. He then, to my great surprise, used his nose to smell the child. Some time later I asked him what he had been doing. He answered that "little children cannot tell us in words where they hurt. So I must use all my senses to find out what has made the child sick."

This small episode carried a fundamentally important message for me and often during my studies of psychology have I thought of my grandfather. I had experienced in him not only a person capable of careful observation but also a person who had enormous respect for nature and a deep and religiously grounded trust in nature in us and around us.

During psychotherapy, both adults and children often discover the 'small child' in them who cannot say 'where it hurts'. In that instance we must use our powers of observation and figuratively use all of our senses to discover the hidden suffering of the person.

In order to protect my clients and because it would be beyond the scope of the present book I cannot here present complete sandplay processes. Therefore, in the case studies I do present, I wish to concentrate chiefly on points which seem to me to be important and typical for an understanding of sandplay processes. It is a great advantage that sand pictures can be photographed. We can therefore document psychic processes in visual form for the reader. Yet, it is still a difficult undertaking to make psychic processes intelligible to the outsider, primarily because a truly sympathetic understanding of such processes may be possible only if the person has also undergone similar experiences.

I would like to point out that in analytical psychology, the psychological school founded by C.G. Jung, the persons who come to our offices are called 'analysands'. In the original sense of the term, this meant that a verbal analysis would be conducted. However, I use this term for all adults who come to consult me. If in the course of this book I speak of the 'analysand', I mean to include both women and men, even if I do not always use both masculine and feminine pronouns.

The publisher and I have agreed that this book should also be intelligible to a reader who has no specialized knowledge of psychology. I have tried to write in a clear and straightforward style. Those specialized terms I could not avoid using are explained in the glossary.

✧ ✧ ✧ ✧ ✧ ✧ ✧ ✧ ✧ ✧ ✧

Acknowledgements

I was a student of Dora M. Kalff's when she was practicing in Zollikon, Switzerland. First I was an 'analysand', undergoing my own sandplay process, and following that experience, I learned through practicing sandplay therapies with other clients. I owe much to Dora Kalff, who not only introduced me to this extraordinarily valuable method but also gave me the basic knowledge necessary for understanding the course of sandplay processes and the therapeutic orientation of the analyst.

Here I would like to thank Dr. Hildegard Milberg of Kösel Publishers, who suggested that this book be written and encouraged me throughout. I should also like to thank Mrs. M.L. Mahdi of Open Court Publishing Company for insisting that this book be translated into English and for her editorial support and assistance. I would also like to thank my translator, Mr. Wolf-Dieter Peter Rainer for his careful, sensitive rendering of the original German text into readable English prose.

I would especially like to thank Eva, Maria, and Elizabeth, and all those analysands who have permitted the use of the slides of their sand pictures. Without the photographic reproductions this book would not have been possible. A world of thanks goes to my children for their patient and loving support, and especially to my brother, Peter Ammann, who accompanied the evolution of this work with his critical and constructive support. Last, I would like to thank James Jarrett and Louise Mahdi who read and corrected the English translation.

CHAPTER ONE

An Introduction to Sandplay as Therapy

The classical form of therapy in the psychology of C.G. Jung is working with dreams. What takes place during such an analysis is a confrontation between the conscious mind of a person and his or her unconscious. The latter manifests itself not only in dreams and body reactions, but also in visions, pictures, or various other imaginative activities. In dialogue with the analysand, the analyst tries to clarify and interpret such expressions of the unconscious. In this way, the analyst offers the analysand access to hitherto unconscious and unknown aspects of his personality as well as to the contents of the collective unconscious which go beyond the individual situation. Both analyst and analysand also work on the phenomena of the 'transference' and 'countertransference' which arise from the unique context of their close co-operation. A Jungian analysis is a process which affects and challenges both analyst and analysand.

The analytic process, however, because it is a *verbal* form of therapy, occurs primarily in dialogue between the analyst and the analysand. It must be understood that the personality of the analyst can influence the course of the analysis in a very specific way by virtue of the strength and power of the word. The analysand can use his verbal abilities to good effect or he can misuse them in order to hide his real being behind them. Language is *one* possibility of human expression and is primarily connected with the rational side of consciousness.

The way a person speaks to us gives us insight into his mental attitudes, the way he thinks. For most people, however, to express their feelings in words is difficult unless they happen to be especially gifted in this way.

Sometimes, feelings of pleasure and pain as well as rage or love grip the entire person, including the body. But just as often the body reacts some time before we become conscious of an emotion having taken hold of us, let alone knowing what our emotion is and what caused it. For example, a person can become paralyzed with fear, the body appearing rigid, hard, cold, and lifeless. To every outside observer it is clear: that person is experiencing fear. But the person

Illustration 1

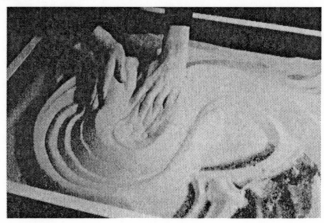

The Hands as Mediator between Spirit and Matter

concerned may lack the words to express verbally what triggered his fear because he is unconscious of what caused it. Perhaps his hands can give form and shape to what is 'unconscious' thereby making it visible and even recognizable in a picture, sandplay, or some other creative medium.

The deeper the emotions and feelings are covered up, the more distanced from consciousness memories and a part of our personality have become, the less likely it is that we can find the words to express them.

We are speechless, but we still have other means of expression. Through dancing, singing, painting, or forming some medium with our hands, we can give expression to what is stirring in us. We can find a connection to our fellow human beings not only through language but also with the body, especially through our hands. The hands can build the bridge between our inner world and the external world. We can pet and caress or hit with our hands, we can do work with them, rework something, transform and give creative expression through them. The hands are the mediators between spirit and matter, between an inner image and an actual creation. By handling, the existing energies become visible.

The fact that the hands can give shape to the powers active in the unconscious, that they can connect the inner and the outer, spirit and matter, is the reason for using sandplay as therapy. In sandplay one is actively engaged, one does not talk much. There is no immediate and rational interpretation of the sand pictures. In the protected frame of the sand tray which holds the unfolding events, a frame

Illustration 2

Microcosm: Sand Picture by a 42-year-old Woman

which has the dimension of approximately 50 × 70 cm (19.6 × 27.5 inches), the analysand shapes with dry or moistened sand and many available small figures his personal world as it is constellated at that time. He models his personal microcosm (see Illustration 2). The miniature figures represent the powers active in him at the time of making the sand picture.

The analyst's role during the production of a sand picture is primarily that of an observer. He sketches and photographs the sand picture. He lets the analysand tell him what comes to mind about the picture and what moved or even shook him while making it. Both analyst and analysand study the sand picture most carefully. The analyst points out what he *sees* in it, *but for the most part does not interpret it at this point*. What is most important is that after the hour is over, the analysand takes the picture of his microcosm, *his world*, inwardly with him. There, it will produce an emotional after-effect which lasts till the next hour, when he may form a new picture. The sand picture should be cleared away by the analyst after the hour. It should not remain in the outer world because it is the energy of the inner image which is important. The Navajo sand paintings used for healing are also taken apart at sunset.

It would not be correct to interpret the sand picture immediately after its creation. The danger lies in fixing the picture's interpretation intellectually, which interrupts the flow of emotions and feelings attending and following its creation. The analysand might say, 'Oh yes, that's it; that's my situation!' But that's *not it*, yet, it is still *becoming* something new. The individual sand pictures only represent the stages in a long, psychic process of transformation which should in no case be disturbed or blocked by interpretations. During this phase of therapy the task of the analyst consists in recognizing what is going on in the analysand, in protecting and supporting this process, in intervening in an emergency, but first and foremost, his task is just to add only so much commentary that the process in the analysand is kept going. To speak in an image: the flames on which the vessel containing the psychic process of the analysand is cooking must be carefully tended by the analyst. The fire mustn't go out. But neither should the flames flare too vigorously lest the contents of the pot boil over or be ruined in some other way.

I would like to add, however, that a similar careful attitude in the analyst also has its place during a verbal analysis. There too, one should only interpret to the degree that the analysand does not feel himself run over but rather feels supported and promoted in his process.

The interpretation of sand pictures can be treated in different ways. This depends on the ongoing therapeutic process in the analysand. In my experience I have found that there are two fundamentally different kinds of process: The *healing process* and the *process of transformation* of the personal worldview.

The *healing process* in sandplay can occur in persons who suffer from psychic disturbances or injuries originating before birth or in early childhood. These people suffer from a so-called disturbance of the primary relationship with the mother or mother-figure which makes it impossible for them to grow up with a healthy trust in the world or in their own life process. In such cases the therapeutic process leads into the deep-seated layers of experience of early childhood. These layers are beyond consciousness and verbalization. Psychic energy then flows back until it reaches the healthy core of the psyche. The pictures and powers of undisturbed wholeness are animated and become effective through sandplay and a healthy foundation is formed on which the new structure of the personality is built (see Chapter 7).[5]

During the healing process, the analysand experiences very strongly these transformations in his being. An immediate interpretation or even one which follows at a later point would be superfluous or disturbing. This is especially the case for children and those adults who cannot or do not want to achieve a rational consciousness of their psychic process. With others, but especially with students who are undergoing a training analysis, it is important, after the process of transformation has run its course (for example, when a new level of development has been reached), to look at, work through and interpret the series of sand pictures, just as we would do with a dream series. And indeed, I have had the impressive experience with

Illustration 3

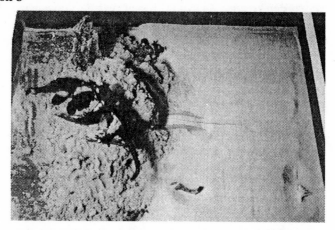

Sand Picture by a 40-year-old Woman. To the right is the light, smooth, intellectual world. The thread of life leads to the left across the bridge to the upturned world of the Shadow which contains dark monsters.

many analysands that after the process has run its course—which can, however, take months—they themselves are capable of interpreting their sand pictures meaningfully. They have experienced the healing powers which have resulted from their creative activity and this experience has effected inner growth and maturation.

The *process of transformation* runs a different course. Here we are dealing with persons who have a fundamentally healthy foundation in life and a stable ego, but whose worldview is too narrow, one-sided, or disturbing. They sense that something is wrong with them, they are restless or distressed, perhaps even depressed or downright sick. Some sense very clearly (perhaps even from their dreams) that a transformation is being prepared within or that an expansion of consciousness is necessary, and enter the process consciously, not simply driven by their unconscious suffering.

The process of transformation includes, for example, fundamental confrontations with the Shadow (see Illustration 3), transformation of the feminine (see Chapter 8), encounter with the Self as an image of God, and so forth. Such psychic transformations which change the basic worldview of a person presuppose a healthy ego consciousness and feelings of self-worth. They represent steps in the process of individuation.

In such cases the analysand will try to come to understand each of his sand pictures, and work out and make conscious their meaning. The analyst can then introduce his own view of a sand picture and cautiously try to formulate an interpretation. But here, too, reticence is in order because we cannot forget that the superseded worldview must be dissolved and left behind before a new one can form. The analyst may, because of his long experience, have an inkling of the shape of the new worldview, but he should never, by incautious interpretation, hinder the emergence of an unforeseen solution. After the process has ended it seems to me to be important in these cases carefully to work through the slides.

Thus, during sandplay by using one's hands creatively, the holistic transformative process which includes both psyche and body is primarily nonverbal and is interpreted verbally only at a later phase according to the insights of analytical psychology. During the initial nonverbal and noninterpretive phase, the analyst maintains a protective, supportive, nonverbal and understanding attitude. He concentrates completely on the process of his analysand and transmits to him his confidence in the self-healing process of the psyche by virtue of what he, as an analyst, is, and not by virtue of what he says.[6] These quiet periods during the therapeutic hour where nothing is spoken are extraordinarily meaningful and valuable. It is not a silence of embarrassment but a conscious silence. Both analyst and analysand direct their attention to the inner world of the analysand leading to a greater understanding.

In the subsequent interpretative discussion of the slides, the analyst becomes more a partner in helping the analysand to understand and find meaning in them so that the pictures in the sand are connected to the experience of the analysand.

One could call these two distinct therapeutic attitudes of the analyst maternal or paternal, or matriarchal or patriarchal. Kathrin Asper differentiates between a mother-specific and a father-specific therapeutic attitude.[7] I prefer not to use these distinctions because they invariable evoke gender-specific roles. As an analyst I feel myself to be neither motherly nor fatherly, but my attitude toward the analysand depends on what seems needed in his process. During the creative formative phase what become active in me are the more instinctual, physical reactions. These depend on subtle sensory perceptions, body feelings, and intuition and on an empathic, emotional relationship with the analysand. This does not happen unconsciously but rather from a conscious turning toward this more receptive attitude which can grip the whole person. When we subsequently enter the more interpretive-analytical process, we call on the more clearly discerning and ordering faculties, such as reason as well as feeling in its subjective valuing function.

Perhaps these two distinctive attitudes can best be elucidated by drawing attention to the various functions of the two cerebral hemispheres.[8] The right hemisphere (which affects the left side of the body), works with holistic, nonverbal images and plays a large role in the processing of emotional information. It seems to me to be significant that the body image is located in the right hemisphere.

The left hemisphere (which affects the right side of the body) is language-oriented and connected with logical and goal-oriented thinking. This hemisphere works rationally and analytically.

The two therapeutic attitudes I have described involve the two hemispheres of the brain alternately, at times drawing more on the functions of the left side, at times more on those of the right side. Use of either one or the other is not better or worse, but depends on the particular requirements of the therapeutic process. During the processes in which we strive for a transformation of the worldview, both attitudes are used more or less simultaneously and in balance.

The balanced use of both hemispheres of the brain has not only a positive effect on the analysand but is essential for the spiritual, psychological, and physical health of the analyst as well. It has been my experience that on days where I use both sandplay therapy and classical dream analysis alternately, I am less tired than on days where one verbal analysis follows another. This is one of the reasons why I should like to see more attention given to the method of sandplay among Jungian analysts. Then not only painted pictures would come into use during a verbal analysis, but an actual method would be available for processes which demand treatment on the nonverbal and emotional level where the formation of images is most appropriate.

If we sketch these two approaches to the therapeutic process and their results briefly from the point of view of the analysand, we can note the following: During the initial formative phase the analysand is led away from critical, rational consciousness. Habitual abstract intellectual thinking which is not related to reality but which has been fostered in most people is purposely avoided by the method itself. What is activated, rather, is the power of the imagination and the sensation function, that is the senses and especially the sense of touch. The power of the imagination and its connection to reality unite while activating the emotions and feelings and form the image of the sand picture. Later I will treat in greater detail this subtle co-ordination of the imagination, the body, matter, and the emotions (see Chapter 4).

In the second phase which follows and during which we work analytically on the sand pictures, we activate the faculty of observation in the analysand. He must fix all the figures in their positions and mutual relatedness and then evaluate this information with both his feelings and his thoughts. This kind of thinking is now not alienated from reality or influenced by the opinions of others, but it is particularly directed toward what is present in the picture and what the analysand has actually experienced through it.

Various levels of being are activated in an analysand during sandplay because it shows the way toward development by either enhancing or retarding certain possibilities and abilities in confronting conscious and unconscious images.

The analysand should approach sandplay with his entire being, both psychically and physically, with total devotion to what he is doing and to what is happening to him. For sandplay is both serious and meaningful. In a limited space, the client presents his world. The term 'world technique' for this method of therapy would also be correct. Yet 'sandplay' denotes the idea of 'playing' with the sand and thus expresses beautifully the connection to the psyche, in that the sand in its dry form has the flowing, rippling properties of water, but in its moist form it is firm and can be molded like earth.

Like psychic life itself, the sand is both energy while moving and energy at rest. There are times during which we are restless and searching, when the stones which build up the structure of our personality are not as well-fitting as they once might have been, when our ideas and values are on shaky ground and are changing. In such times we are 'homeless'; everything is in flux and we really are 'on the road'. After such phases of unrest we begin once again to put things in order. Our house of the soul is being built anew, perhaps with new building blocks or perhaps with the old, newly placed and fitted. We have found a new life form which will give us a sense of peace and balance for some time to come—until such time that from the depth of the soul the archetype of the Self once again constellates a change and introduces a new process of transformation.

Sand and psyche have much in common. No other material I know of represents psychic energy so well: flowing, moving, it searches for form. It finds a new form—and from there it begins to flow again.

The person who stands at the sand tray and creatively forms the sand is totally immersed in what he is doing. This direct interplay of body and psyche is not generally attained during classical dream analysis. With both methods, it is of decisive importance that the insights from the analysis will be translated into the reality of everyday life. But besides working through the phenomenon of transference and countertransference which might arise, the analyst has relatively little observational knowledge of his client's outer reality. The analyst is dependent on the client's description of his everyday life as well as on his honesty.

In classical dream analysis the analyst is also dependent on his client's ability to remember when he tells his dreams. It happens time and again that important dreams are 'forgotten' or censored during narration. Moreover, it is nearly an art in itself for a client to tell a dream in such a way that the analyst can truly *feel* his way into it without interjecting his own fantasies. There is yet another danger in retelling a dream: we may miss the color and the feeling-tone of the dream experience when an interpretation of the dream message is desired too quickly.

In sandplay things are slightly different. The danger of biased evaluation is small because the analysand usually does not know what a 'good' or a 'bad' sand picture might look like. Also, because he is present at the very time of the sandplay, the analyst can concentrate on every detail in the sand tray and observe every movement of the analysand during the entire hour. This presupposes, of course, that the analyst is able—objectively and precisely—to listen, feel, and observe. In this way he can get exact information concerning the condition of his analysand. It should be recalled that the analysand more or less unconsciously forms his pictures in the sand tray and therefore is often not conscious of which figure he used where. If the analyst knows which unconscious condition is expressed in the picture of the analysand, he can effect much by merely calling attention to the individual figures and their position. In my opinion it is most important that analyst and analysand view the completed picture together and in detail. The analysand becomes accountable for what he has put in his picture and learns to see the individual elements of his sand picture in their mutual relatedness. He attempts to orient himself in his own 'world picture', not, at first, through interpretation, but rather by careful observation.

The subtle use of one's senses and precise observation of reality is an indispensable precondition for securely anchoring oneself in this world; for outer, concrete reality has an enormous impact on the inner, psychic world. We are quite used to the thought that the inner, psychic-spiritual world expresses itself—perhaps even 'incarnates' itself—in outer reality, but the reverse is equally true. Nature and the environment man has created also affect the psyche. There is a constant exchange between inner and outer, between psyche and environment.[10]

For example, having a deep and instinctual knowledge of the course of the seasons and the dying blossoming of nature gives us an understanding of order and regularity. This in turn offers us a sense of security and orientation. One becomes more conscious of the fact that natural cycles foster the process of becoming. Those familiar with the nature of growth understand that there can be no impatience or hurrying it along. This holds true whether we mean the growth of a creative work or the renewal of a worldview, perhaps even an

analysis or a pregnancy. Those who are more conscious will tend that
which is newly emerging with more patience and attention. But in
today's society, isn't it exactly the opposite? We have lost our
relationship to nature. How many pregnant women cannot or will
not—psychically and physically—give the unborn child the peaceful
and healthy space which it needs for its development?

I have mentioned that many persons who come for help suffer
from a disturbance of the primary relationship to the mother. Often
this begins at a very early stage—even during the mother's pregnancy. During early childhood the mother or person with whom a
primary relationship can be formed represents the most important
contact with the world; as a matter of fact, that person *is* the world
for the child. How can the child receive a sense of security and trust
in the world and in his own life, if that person does not have a good
or trusting relationship to his or her own nature?

Not knowing or being indifferent to certain processes of nature—
and I would include in these, for example, knowledge of the orbits of
the sun and the moon, the position of the stars—has, it seems to me,
a negative effect on the sense of the person's primal trust in his own
life in this world. Does it not seem natural that a young person
should observe and get to know the own foundation of his life,
namely his own body and its immediate environment as well as the
plant and animal world of his larger environment, his ecosystem,
before he would turn to abstract knowledge and technology? I feel
strongly that it isn't enough to love one's child, to feed it and protect
it. A good mother or father must introduce the child to the essentials
of 'Mother Nature's nature', both inwardly and outwardly. A child
can never learn in school how to trust in his own soul and body, or
gain knowledge concerning health and disease, or his own sexuality;
this knowledge must be mediated by the parents through their
example in everyday life.

This disregard or even disdain of the seemingly self-evident,
unspectacular natural processes also spills over—harmfully, I should
say—to the human body. The body becomes the less-regarded sister
of the mind, which is clearly privileged. Here I don't mean the body
in the sense of its being an object of exhibition for fitness and beauty;
rather I mean the body as a part of our wholeness and as it relates to
the other concrete things of this world, subject to its laws of growth
and decay.

One could say that the body is held in lesser esteem. Or, to state
this even more strongly: there is a disastrous severance of the mind
from its earthly, human conditionality. One can observe this severed-
ness in fantasies as well as in different forms of behavior: for example
in drug- or alcohol-induced intoxication, or in habitual endless talk

or daydreaming, or in certain psychological practices which only result in an inflated personality structure. One can assume that such persons wish to escape from their unsatisfactory lives. It is for such reasons that during therapy we must neither neglect the concrete environment nor the body as the carrier of the material part of the wholeness of our personality. Otherwise we run the risk of a split between the abstract, the spiritual and the concrete, material world. There is, as I have stated, a constant exchange and reciprocal action between the spiritual and the material world. To neglect the one results in a deficit in the other. When we carefully pay attention to one of the two aspects we thereby enhance the other as well.

I spoke earlier of the course of the sun and the position of the stars. In certain fairy tales, the hero or heroine seeks help through orientation with the sun or moon or stars. Let me illustrate the importance of such facts in our daily lives with a small example. A nine-year-old boy came for therapy because he suffered from deep anxieties. He feared, among other things, that he would get lost in the big city where I have my practice and be unable to find his way home again. Of course, his anxieties were also, but not only, an expression of his sense of being lost inwardly. I drew an approximate plan of the city in the sand. We then laid a cross with the four cardinal points marked on the sand. He understood that his home was somewhat east of my office, but how could he know which way was East? We observed and talked about the properties of the four seasons and the

Illustration 4

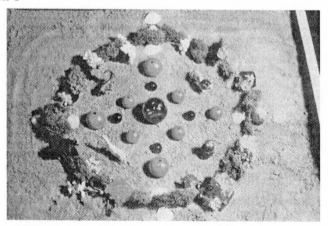

Garden of the Soul: Sand Picture by a 42-year-old Woman

path of the sun in the course of the day and related this to the changing seasons. Very quickly, the boy discovered how to locate the southerly direction and, to derive from this, where East must be. And at night, when the sun did not shine? He observed—something he learned with his father—that there is a certain star which always shows where North is. Such experiences with the sun and stars came as a great relief to the boy. They gave his young personality—in such a big world—a growing sense of security.

This example may seem insignificant but how many adults know in which direction the window of the living-room faces? Which plants, birds, and insects live in their garden? And how many know the garden of their soul?

A sand picture can also be seen as the garden of one's soul where the inner and the outer come together. Here, in protected space, a person can learn to watch and recognize the reciprocal action between the inner and the outer world.

In order to underscore the extraordinary importance of the role nature plays in the human soul, I should like to cite Laurens van der Post, the great author and expert on both inner and outer nature:

> If we were to investigate the history of Europe, the civilization in which are rooted most of our values, we would find that over time a disastrous split has occurred in human culture. The more rational we became, the more we have lost contact with a primordial trust, 'to be known', and a feeling of belonging. This split has brought on the loss of meaning in our hearts and in our minds.

And then he continues:

> One cause of great misunderstanding in our modern world is the notion that everything in us is subjective and the truly objective world lies outside of us. This is as absurd as it is wrong. We have an immeasurably objective world in us. This is the world with which psychologists today are increasingly preoccupied. They have already discovered that the split, this quasi-schizophrenic psychic condition of today's society is a result of the denial, neglect and exploitation of this inner world, a world which is as extraordinary, objective, and natural as a wilderness can be, the garden of our own soul.
>
> Perhaps the only great man whom I have known, Carl Gustav Jung, told me once how he as a child discovered to his great lament that there are two states of consciousness in the world: one, which he called the natural or country-consciousness and the other which he called the city-consciousness. This second one appeared to him, as it increasingly does to me, to get more unreal, frightening and nightmarish as time goes on. It occasioned in him a longing for a return to the natural or country-consciousness which became ever

greater and more urgent. "The more I became familiar with the frightful life of the city, the stronger became my conviction that what I was getting to know as reality wasn't reality at all, but rather a distortion and degeneration of the human spirit which now claimed to be 'the reality'. I longed for the other reality which appeared to me to be lacking or to having been lost. I had a vision of the world as a country between rivers and forests, with humans and animals, small villages on which the sun shone and clouds moved and which had clear, dark nights—a world, in short, in which splendidly uncertain and unpredictable things could happen. And the world of nature which surrounded us would then be an open landscape, not simply a place on the map but rather God's world which was ordered by him and was filled with secret meaning.[11]

This is how Laurens van der Post writes concerning the effects on the soul when we neglect both our outer and inner nature. Jung's reflections cited by van der Post also speak of the longing for a natural consciousness and the importance which Jung assigned to a free nature filled with meaning and ordered by God.

This introduction to sandplay would, in my opinion, be incomplete without mentioning the conspicuous parallels that exist between sandplay and alchemy. For some time now I have been struck by the importance both methods place on combining the material and concrete operation with the theoretical and psychological elaboration of the process. In alchemy the name given to the concrete operation was the 'operatio' and the theoretical elaboration was called 'theoria'. Together they formed the 'opus', or the *alchemical work*. The imagination plays a large role both in alchemy and in sandplay, and in both methods the imaginative activity follows from the interplay of the material and physical with the psychic components.

In his *Memories, Dreams, Reflections,*[12] Jung, when describing his work on alchemical texts, mentions how quickly he saw the remarkable correspondence between analytical psychology and alchemy. He discovered that the experiences of the alchemists corresponded to his own experiences and that the world of the alchemists was, in a certain sense, his own world as well. He had found, as it were, the historical counterpart to his psychology of the Unconscious and he was able thereby to give his psychology a historical basis. The possibility of comparing analytical psychology with alchemy and seeing a continuity traceable as far back as the gnostic religions during the time of Christ gave his work substance. Jung's researches into these old texts helped him locate his own foundations. Now he was able to place the pictorial world of the imagination and the clinical material which he had gathered from his practice in historical perspective and draw conclusions by ordering these elements in a meaningful way.

Elsewhere[13] Jung writes that alchemy had laid the most essential groundwork for the psychology of the Unconscious. First, because alchemy inadvertently left behind a treasure trove of pictorial material which is of the utmost importance for the modern interpretation of symbols, and second, because alchemy by virtue of its intentionally synthetic endeavors suggests symbolic procedures similar to the dreams of our analysands. Jung continues: the entire alchemical process of opposites can just as easily illustrate the way of individuation of an individual, with the difference that no single person will ever reach the wealth and volume of alchemical symbolism. The advantage of this is that this symbolism has grown through the centuries while the individual case with its short lifespan is subject to a limited experience and expressive ability.

Alchemical symbolism is not only extraordinarily valuable for amplification of dream material, but is most helpful in the interpretation of sand pictures. We can also see parallels between the individual steps in the alchemical process and the psychic processes of transformation, especially of individuation, for the work done in sand. Psychic processes progress in similar, generally valid, patterns. This accounts for the fact that we can find in the basic structures similarities in the way the processes run their course. We can see this not only in the processes and symbols occurring during dream analysis or during sandplay but also in alchemy. The only difference is that each method uses different means and forms.

It seems to me important to refer once again to the alchemical 'work', because we can find there the most important connection with sandplay. Jung in 'Psychology and Alchemy' writes the following concerning this 'work'.

> The basis of alchemy is the work (opus). Part of this work is practical, the *operation* itself, which is to be thought of as a series of experiments with chemical substances. . . . The profound darkness that shrouds the alchemical procedure comes from the fact that although the alchemist was interested in the chemical part of the work he also used it to devise a nomenclature for the psychic transformation that really fascinated him. . . . The method of alchemy, psychologically speaking, is one of boundless amplification. The *amplificatio* is always appropriate when dealing with some obscure experience which is so vaguely adumbrated that it must be enlarged and expanded by being set in a psychological context in order to be understood at all. That is why, in analytical psychology, we resort to amplification in the interpretation of dreams,

Illustration 5

Historical Picture of the Alchemical Work. To the right is the practically acting person (operatio), to the left the conferring abbot, monk, and layman (theoria), and in the middle the alchemical vessel.

for a dream is too slender a hint to be understood until it is enriched by the stuff of association and analogy and thus amplified to the point of intelligibility. This *amplificatio* forms the second part of the *opus*, and is understood by the alchemist as *theoria*.[14]

Illustration 5 graphically illustrates the two interacting sides during the alchemical 'work'. To the right is a man in his laboratory engaged in 'hands-on' labor. He represents the *operation*, the practical activity or operational side of the work. To the left we see three men, an abbot, a monk and a layman conferring together. They represent the *theoria*, the theoretical side of the work. In the middle, on top of the furnace, stands the tripod with the round alchemical vessel, the actual center of action, for in it the slow transformation of the substance occurs.

Text and picture seem to me to express clearly the relationship between alchemy and sandplay. For sandplay too joins the *operatio*, the practical work at the sand tray, and *theoria*, the theoretical elaboration of the action. We can think of the sand tray, figuratively, as the alchemical vessel in which the transformation of the psychic substance occurs. Here is the protected space, a kind of uterus or maternal womb in which a holistic renewal and rebirth is made possible. This renewal takes shape through the healing and transforming power of the imagination.

Practical Considerations:
the Sandplay Method in Action

I mentioned in the introduction that sandplay is a hands-on method. In the center of the sandplay-room, we have a sand tray at about table height with the dimensions of 22.5 × 28.5 inches (57 × 72 cm) which corresponds to the field of vision of the person standing in front of the tray. The tray is about three inches deep and is filled with fine sand. We can now work down into the sand or build it up to a considerable height. The bottom of the tray is painted blue so that we can, if we desire, create an illusion of water at the bottom of the tray. Of course, we can mix the sand with real water in order to shape it better or create, for example, various wet landscapes such as swamp or marsh. Because sand does not dry from one hour to the next it is a good idea to have two sand trays in the room in order to have dry sand on hand at all times.

In addition, the therapy room should have a wide variety of miniature figures, people from various historical periods and in various functions, animals, trees, plants, flowers, houses and their corresponding implements, sacred buildings and religious symbols, bridges, cars, and much else; but also rocks, wood, glass marbles and colored glass stones, seashells, and other kinds of raw materials to be able to make what is not readily available. One can never have all the desired figures but this can be an incentive for the analysand to create his own. What really counts is not the total number of figures but rather that the available figures have symbolic value. It is important that there are not just light, friendly, beautiful objects but that ugly, dark, evil, and fearsome things are represented too. Just as important are symbolic figures from foreign cultures in order to illustrate the 'wholly other', the strange and foreign in the psyche.

The analysand expresses in the sand what is spontaneously constellated in him during that hour. He is completely free to play or not to play with the sand, just as he likes. The analyst gives him no instructions. Figures can be used if it seems necessary but some adults only sculpt with the sand.

Some therapists have criticized the rectangular form of the tray and have suggested that the tray should be a square or a circle

Illustration 6

The Sand Tray in the Room

because such forms enhance psychic concentration and centering. In my opinion this would be completely wrong. Just imagine the totally different effects which either a square, circular, or rectangular room have on a person. Because of the inequality of measurements the rectangular space creates tension, unrest, and a desire for movement, a desire to go forward. The square or circular space, however, creates balance, rest, concentration toward the center. It is possible to compare the analytic process with a constant search for the center in uncentered space. At times a person stands too far to the right, at times too far to the left, or he vacillates between too high or too deep (which expresses itself in the rectangular sand tray through the fact that the analysand works distinctly upward or outward to the sides), until he finally finds his center, his personal circle, in the rectangle of the sand tray.

Here I would like to add some reflections on the space of the sand tray. At the beginning of the hour the analysand finds the tray

Illustration 7

Miniature Figures

neutral, only filled with lightly smoothed-over sand. We all know
that human expression needs space to express itself. And the reverse
is true too: empty spaces allow for life to be created, they tempt the
person to fill the empty space with life.[15]

Let us take some simple examples. We place an empty piece of
paper in front of a child and offer him some crayons. Normally the
child will begin to draw without any hesitation. It is the same if we
give the child a sand tray and some figures. The child quickly begins
to play with the sand and starts to build mountains and valleys, lakes
and forests, create streets and houses, puts people and animals in
place until the empty space is filled with life. All of this will happen
provided the child is allowed simply to play without being required
to achieve anything. If this is the case, then the untouched sand tray
will soon be filled with the lively pictures of the inner world of the
child. These pictures are simply there, they wish to flow outward,
they only need a space in which to be expressed. That is why children

Illustration 8

A Frightening Image Appears in the Sand

with psychic difficulties are almost magically drawn to the sand tray in the therapy room.

Not only children but adults as well need empty spaces of all kinds in order to express their fantasies and give shape to their inner pictures. The narrowness and congestion of our life spaces, which do not allow for change or renewal, are enemies of fantasy and the life process. This is not only true for the outer world but in a figurative sense also for the life spaces of the soul. Our heads are crammed with knowledge and information of all kinds, the ears with street noise, radio noise, and inner noise, and our hearts with pent-up emotions and feelings.

It is perfectly understandable, therefore, that even adults are spontaneously drawn to the untouched sand tray where everything is still possible. Some adults and children begin to form the picture freely and without the pressure to perform. But in case we forget: persons seeking psychotherapeutic help often cannot express themselves at the sand tray freely and easily. They are afraid of the untouched sand tray or an empty piece of paper because out of such emptiness they are afraid that their own shadow figures, demonic shapes, or very frightening images may appear to them.

Narcissistically disturbed persons have a tendency to see their delusions of grandeur grow into infinity and explode the frame of what is for them meaningful and realizable. It is for this reason that the sand tray is limited to a specific size. It is a manageable size; one can see the whole tray at a glance, avoiding the overflow of fantasies.

In any case, the sand tray has great appeal for children and adults because both have a deep human need to express and shape their world. They perceive sandplay as creative, beneficial and healing. But some people especially at the beginning, experience some fear as they come to the sand tray.

The sand tray, as the vessel in which the psychic transformation occurs, can be equated with the hermetic vessel of the alchemists, which they called the 'vas hermeticum'. This vessel or 'krater' is a feminine symbol and originally meant a vessel filled with spirit which had been sent down to earth by the creator-god in order that those who aspire to higher consciousness could be baptized in it. It was a kind of uterus of spiritual renewal and rebirth. This immersion into something alien, however, seems frightening at first.

The analysand can overcome this fear and enter the therapeutic process with trust and confidence only in an environment which Dora Kalff calls the "free and protected space". She writes with reference to the child in therapy:

> This free space occurs in the therapeutic situation when the therapist is able to accept the child fully, so that he or she, as a person, is a part of everything going on in the room just as much as is the child himself. When a child feels that he is not alone—not only in his distress but also in his happiness—he then feels free but still protected, in all his expressions. Why is this relationship of confidence so important? Under certain circumstances, the situation of the first phase, the one of the mother-child unity, can be restored. This psychic situation can establish an inner peace which contains the potential for the development of the total personality, including its intellectual and spiritual aspects.
>
> It is the role of the therapist to perceive these powers and, like the guardian of a precious treasure, protect them in their development. For the child, the therapist represents as a guardian, the space, the freedom and at the same time, the boundaries.[16]

This is a beautiful description, it seems to me, of the broad significance of the 'free and protected space' and can serve just as well as a description of the therapeutic attitude which the analyst must have toward adult analysands. Let me state once again that the dimensions of the sand tray, inclusive as they are of the area of the visual field, are a good human measure, in that by providing limits the analysand can focus and concentrate better. The limited size of the tray makes it possible for the analyst to recognize and order at a glance the diverse, confusing and often contradictory elements of a sand picture. I greatly value being able to concentrate on this visual field because, for one thing, much energy remains available to take in other information. For example, I listen to what the analysand tells

Illustration 9

Sand Picture by a 35-year-old Male, working in a decidedly meditative mode

me about the sand picture or what he might say about the experiences of daily life. I try to intuit how the analysand experiences himself physically at the moment or I can think about the meaning of what is happening in the sand. On the other hand, during important moments, I can focus all my energies completely on the events in the sand tray. For, after all, that is the focal point of the therapeutic process and of the relationship between the analysand and the analyst.

One might ask why the material we use in the sand tray is sand rather than potter's clay. A female analysand once told me something quite beautiful in this connection. She said "Stones are primordial matter. Sand is matter ground by the infinity of time. It makes one mindful of eternity. Sand is matter which has been transformed and has almost become liquid and spiritual." And indeed! Sand in its dry form purls and is almost liquid. It is light and when we touch it with our hands it feels soft and sensitive.

When we move our hands through the dry sand, patterns are left as ripples in water. We can also blow the sand, creating delicate formations as only the wind and the sand can compose, and they evoke images of the desert (see Illustrations 9 and 10). Playing with dry sand is releasing and reminds one not only of childhood play but perhaps also of the gentle and tender touch of one's mother or some other dear person. But others, just by touching the sand experience a great sadness. They may even cry convulsively because they are suddenly reminded of their great desire to be touched and to gently touch someone else. The intimate physical touching between mother

Illustration 10

Sand Picture by a 40-year-old Male

and child plays an extraordinary role in the well-being and growth of the child. And in later life as well, people long for physical closeness and loving touching.

When mixed with water, the sand gets ever darker and begins to take on the quality of earth. The sand becomes firm and may be formed or shaped. Now we can create landscapes or three-dimensional structures of all kinds (see Illustration 11). (I should mention here that those who do not know their own darker, more shadowy side or will not admit it, often have difficulty working three-dimensionally.) But the sand pictures or sculptures do not remain. They do not become firmer and more nearly permanent as they dry, as would, for example, a figure made of clay. In a short time the sand sculpture falls apart and disintegrates.

And it is exactly this which seems to me very important: sand pictures are not works of art which should live permanently, even if, at the time, we find them very beautiful and impressive. They should not remain fixed in the external world. They are images of the soul made visible; every analysand (and, incidentally, the analyst as well!) carries them within after the hour, where their effect lingers and acts upon the psyche. A transformation may take place. This would manifest itself later in a new picture. In the sand tray the picture falls apart: the analyst clears it away. One could also say that what the analysand is presented with at each hour—at the tray—is an unformed world out of which he can form his individual world. In his soul he carries this image with him, but in the tray it will pass. The sand becomes again an unformed, unintentional world. The inner

Illustration 11

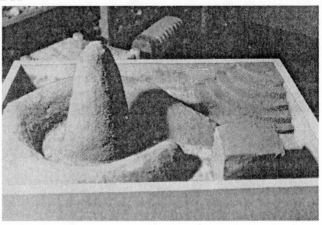

Sand Picture by a 38-year-old Male

world in which he carries his picture is for him just as real as our external world, the so-called world of objects. Actually, because of its infinity and eternity, the inner world is more real. How appropriate the sand is: it is the best medium to give three-dimensional representation to both the inner and the outer, as they undergo constant change. As my analysand put it: "Sand is matter ground by the infinity of time. It makes one mindful of eternity . . ." The outer world is extraordinarily important for the formation of the inner picture, yet only the latter becomes active in the psyche.

For his own documentation and control of the therapeutic process, the analyst should sketch every sand picture, note all that is of importance, and take one or more photographic slides of it. It is important that the slide be taken from the analysand's position so that the diagram I have included (page 48, below) can serve as an aid for the interpretation of the symbolic aspects of spatial phenomena. Just as important, it seems to me, is to note the actual source of light during sandplay. When taking the slide, the analyst should recreate this source by placing the photo floodlamp at the appropriate location because it often happens that figures which are placed in the shadow are actually meant by the analysand to represent his shadowy parts (see Illustration 36). Flashbulbs are not suitable for photographing because important shadows become blurred, making it difficult to recognize the structures. Often, the structure of the sand, as foundational element, is just as expressive as the figures which might be placed upon it.

CHAPTER THREE

Why are Sand Pictures Necessary?

In the previous chapter I have described the materials available to the analysand during sandplay. But why do we want such pictures? Why do we wish to activate or reactivate these mostly unconscious psychic images and states of being, and make them visible in the sand? In order to elucidate this point, I need to make some comments concerning our understanding of consciousness and what we call the unconscious.

Every person perceives at some time or other that his total personality includes much more than the small part of himself that he knows consciously. And it is just the same with the world and the universe. The more we know of it consciously, the more we recognize how much we do not know. Just as we are part of the cosmos as a conscious being, our unconscious side is interwoven with the collective unconscious.

Most persons recognize in themselves or in others that there are different kinds of consciousness. We know a sober, rather emotionless consciousness which consists primarily of clearly intelligible facts and which expresses itself in systematic, logical thoughts. This is our rational consciousness.

But we also know a consciousness which is much more difficult to describe. It is one which is made up more of images, emotions, feelings and intuitions, not level-headed or matter-of-fact, but full of ambiguity and flowing. This kind of consciousness does not seek a linear goal, rather it seeks to slowly interweave the myriad bits of information it perceives from the outer and inner world to form a global picture. Such a consciousness may seem muddy and diffuse, but it need not be so. The ego of a person can be quite balanced and stable while he is in this state of consciousness. But it takes much more time, patience, and empathy to listen to such a person and make contact with his psyche.

It has often been said that women's consciousness is ambiguous and diffuse and that they do not think logically. This may indeed be the case with some women, but that is no reason to give it a negative value. There is much more color, abundance, and comprehensiveness in grasping things and interweaving them in a more global manner. One can hear intermediate and incidental tones, lost thoughts can be recalled and newly rising intuitions taken in. This pictorial and imaginative consciousness lies closer to the unconscious, the creative foundation of the soul. It is therefore more spontaneous, fluid, and lively than rational consciousness, which is often concerned with mere facts.

Furthermore, there is also our body consciousness, which is most difficult to describe in words. To describe a level of consciousness correctly would require that we speak of it in its own terms or in terms germane to it. Body consciousness can be experienced and expressed appropriately only with the body, quite obviously in dance, and in more hidden ways during our everyday activity when we physically move and experience ourselves. The very subtle network of perceiving and expressing our instincts also belongs here. For example, we can experience this body consciousness in an intimate love relationship or in the early mother-child relationship when this very subtle, nonverbal, and non-imagistic exchange of bodily energies takes place. It is not without reason that the mother or father carries the child snuggled near the heart and the belly because it is there near the peritoneum that we experience the center of body consciousness.

The different kinds of consciousness which I have described are more developed in some persons, for example, more consciously available to them. In others they can be pre-conscious, unconscious, atrophied, or injured, but in any case no longer at their disposal, although often still capable of development. In the therapeutic method of sandplay we first—during the creative phase—appeal to and develop body consciousness as well as the pictoral and imaginative consciousness. Later, when we interpret the sand pictures we develop our rational consciousness.

But what do we mean by the unconscious, which is often called the 'subconscious'? The unconscious does not consist of the 'subconscious', that is, of something which lies below consciousness, even though we often treat it as if it were inferior, or as if we needed to put it down or suppress it. The unconscious comes to meet us from all sides: from matter whose spirit we do not know, from our own body and our psyche whose essence we cannot intuit or penetrate, from the universe whose coherence and laws we do not grasp, and from the collective psyche, whose unconscious side we call the collective unconscious. As the name of the concept implies, the unconscious is all that of which we are not conscious and of whose existence we have perhaps only a small inkling or none at all. Nonetheless, it is still there and has effects in the real world.

Just how many things are not present to a person, while they nonetheless objectively exist—because one is unconscious of them—

can be illustrated by a small example from my practice. Often an analysand will say: 'You've bought quite a few new sandplay figures. I haven't seen this one and that one. That one is new!' Most of the time I have to tell them that the figures aren't new at all but have been standing on the shelves for years. Then my analysands are quite astonished that things which were objectively present were not present for them, because they had not seen them consciously.

This means that a person can really only see, both within and without, that of which he is conscious. But, of course, parents, teachers or therapists can stimulate the process of becoming conscious by pointing out outer realities at the appropriate times. This is the reason why precise and detailed observation of the sand picture is so very important: the external realities can become psychic realities.

Thus, the unconscious is an infinite stream of realities which are not (or not yet or no longer) perceived by our consciousness. The personal unconscious contains materials which have been acquired during the individual's life. These contents can be recognized as personal because their source can be discovered in our personal past. The attributes belonging to mankind in general Jung called the collective unconscious. This foundation of the human psyche is the fertile soil, the matrix for consciousness, in which it is rooted and out of which it grows.

A person's psychic reactions including his intellectual abilities are influenced by this primal matrix and infused with energy from clusters of feeling-toned mental images, the so-called complexes which are grouped around a central nucleus. Certain complexes may be acquired through specific life experiences, but many others appear to be inherited structures. This accounts for the fact that without being influenced from outside, people from diverse regions and times will exhibit similar emotions, feelings, mental categories and connections. These general complexes which function as dynamic central nuclei in the human psyche Jung called the archetypes. Through them originate, among other things, symbolic images of the same or a similar kind in widely differing cultures and peoples. Based on the existence of these archetypes and their energetic effects upon the psyche, it can be stated that certain human states and processes always express themselves in similar symbolic images, be it in dream analysis, during sandplay, in fairytales and myths, or in alchemy.

It must be kept in mind that both the personal and the collective psyche have light and dark aspects; that is, they contain constructive, life-furthering as well as destructive and life-negating aspects. The contents of the unconscious can on the one hand be the cause of psychic dissolution as can be seen during a psychosis, or they can exhibit singular healing factors, as can be demonstrated during therapy. It is therefore of great importance how the individual as well as the collective community handles these contents of the unconscious.

Many persons close their minds to influences of the unconscious. This may be caused by the fear that they might not be able to cope with such contents, or by indolence or ignorance, but perhaps also because the person needs a goal-oriented, rational consciousness and must therefore, exclude certain influences of the unconscious. However, when this happens, the healing and complementing powers are excluded as well although they could be needed in maintaining the good state of health of the psyche. Jung formulated this as follows:

> We need the unconscious contents to supplement the conscious attitude. If the conscious attitude were only to a slight degree "directed", the unconscious could flow in quite of its own accord .... Directedness is absolutely necessary for the conscious process, but as we have seen it entails an unavoidable one-sidedness. Since the psyche is a self-regulating system, just as the body is, the regulating counteraction will always develop in the unconscious. Were it not for the directedness of the conscious function, the counteracting influences of the unconscious could set in unhindered. It is just this directedness that excludes them. This, of course, does not inhibit the counteraction, which goes on in spite of everything. Its regulating influence, however, is eliminated by critical attention and the directed will, because the counteraction as such seems incompatible with the conscious direction. To this extent the psyche of civilized man is no longer a self-regulating system . . .[17]

We can see from this statement that, on the one hand, the psyche would be a self-regulating system if the regulating influences of the unconscious were allowed to become effective in a natural way. On the other hand, civilization needs a durable, balanced, and goal-oriented consciousness, which opposes with a certain strength and decisiveness the threatening influences of the unconscious which might be inappropriate at a given time. It is not without reason that for quite some time the left cerebral hemisphere which is linked to this goal-oriented, logical thinking was considered to be the dominant hemisphere and valued correspondingly higher. The imagistic nature of the right hemisphere which is much more connected with the emotions is closer to the unconscious and more irrational and hence undesirable for certain civilizing processes.

For this reason the functions of the right cerebral hemisphere are not inferior but must defer some of their usefulness in favor of civilizing processes. Certain priorities are absolutely essential for the development of the individual as well as for the whole human race, but of course only as long as they enhance development, not inhibit it. As soon as rigidity and stagnation occur in development, the other side must be included again. Figuratively speaking, mankind can hop forward on one leg for some time, in order to exercise it, but after a certain time the other leg will have to be included again, otherwise the balance of wholeness is lost and mankind will be quite crippled.

Most persons do not pay attention to the latent potential present in the unconscious. They simply favor the conscious processes. Thus, impulses and dreams, which are, after all, the most spontaneous expressions of the unconscious, are not perceived or are simply repressed. The regulating function of the unconscious is thereby largely eliminated, but as Jung states, it "goes on in spite of everything". To put it simply, not to pay attention to contents which are important for psychological equilibrium, forces them to find alternate means of expression, perhaps as anxieties, depressions, or through physical symptoms.

The self-regulation of the psyche can be disturbed in early childhood. Children have not yet developed their goal-directed will so the regulating influences of the unconscious should be functioning spontaneously. Yet, because of the initial lack of differentiation of the inner and the outer world, children live in a certain identity with their parents (their family) and are often held back by this identity. The self-regulation of the child gets disturbed by the critical attention and the directedness of the will of the parents, especially as regards the parents' unlived unconscious lives. Later, the school trains the child to be 'on the job'. Although the school must promote the directedness of the will, it sometimes overtaxes the child in this regard.

The potential for self-regulation could still exist during the child's leisure time if he were allowed to express his spontaneous inspirations. But regulated leisure activities are often programmed by the parents rather than by the children themselves.

It is a truly difficult challenge, even for responsible educators, to provide an adequate environment for the child's self-regulation. Education as well as limitation are necessary in order to form and adapt the personality to the environment; at the same time we must allow the child's innermost soul an opportunity to express itself.

Jung writes of the child archetype:

> The "child" . . . . represents the strongest, the most ineluctable urge in every being, namely the urge to realize itself. It is, as it were, an incarnation of the inability to do otherwise, equipped with all the

powers of nature and instinct . . . . The urge and compulsion to self-
realization is a law of nature and thus of invincible power, even
though its effect at the start, is insignificant and improbable.[18]

Here Jung speaks of the archetype whose contents contain much
more than just the child. The 'child' represents the new, the evolving
but also a new attitude of consciousness, a new idea or even a new
cultural era. For example, the Christ-child was the highly-charged
symbol capable of representing that which is new and healing, a
newly evolving religious culture.

But the real child also has an ineluctable urge . . . to realize itself,
just as later in life in the adult we can see the child archetype wishing
to become active. Unfortunately, this immensely powerful energy
which strives toward development and realization is often blocked or
thwarted at an early stage.

In analytical psychology, the process toward development of the
rounded, mature individual personality, is called the process of
individuation. In the Jungian sense, individuation has nothing in
common with an egocentric individuality, rather the contrary. Jung
writes about this as follows:

> Individuation is a natural necessity inasmuch as its prevention by
> a levelling down to collective standards is injurious to the vital
> activity of the individual. Since individuality is a prior psycholog-
> ical and physiological datum, it also expresses itself in psycholog-
> ical ways. Any *serious check* to individuality, therefore, is an
> *artificial stunting*. It is obvious that a social group consisting of
> stunted individuals cannot be a healthy and viable institution; only
> a society that can preserve its internal cohesion and collective
> values, while at the same time granting the individual the greatest
> possible freedom, has any prospect of enduring vitality. As the
> individual is not just a single, separate being, but by his very
> existence presupposes a collective relationship, it follows that the
> process of individuation must lead to more intense and broader
> collective relationships and *not* to *isolation* (emphasis added).[19]

I place great importance on the need for clarity with regard to the
meaning of individuation. It has often been claimed that Jungian
psychology creates nothing but selfish and egocentric individualists.
This can never be the goal of a mature personality because taking
responsibility for relating to the inner life is inextricably bound to a
responsible attitude toward the outer world as well. Besides being
individuals, we participate in diverse intimate relationships or larger
networks as parts of a group or a collective.

Let us return to the insight that the urge to self-realization is the
natural law of every being. Many persons, especially many parents,

cannot accept this. They cannot admit that from the seed of a sunflower must come a sunflower and not a rose even if they stand in front of the plant every day and beg it to become a rose. The child gains a deep confidence in his own life process only if he is allowed to become a 'sunflower'—if there should be one inside him. If the sunflower-child is forced to become a rose, it is the same as if parents or the larger environment cover the child with alien petals or an alien skin under which the original personality atrophies or, worse still, suffocates. This foreign skin consists of projections which the environment has placed on the child, or more aptly put, it consists of projections which bury the real child. There may be some adaptation by the child to this alien skin or even active participation in the production of it; nonetheless, the real individual essence is not perceived under the skin and stands little chance of development.

Therapeutic experience shows that every child carries within the unconscious the knowledge of its psychic potential and its possibilities of healing. The adult too still has this knowledge, only it must be understood that his 'skin armor' has become increasingly impenetrable, and he will have to expend greater time and effort to advance into the depth of the unconscious. But if in the analytic situation we are successful in activating the vital powers of the Self, then there is a good chance for healing and an emerging wholeness of the personality. As an empirical concept, the Self comprises the unity and wholeness of the total conscious and unconscious personality. From it emerge the centering and ordering structures which effect the integration of the person. How these structures become active in the individual, that is, what course is taken by them in order to proceed with development within the actual individual life, can really only be 'known' by that individual. He can experience this development provided that he turns a responsive and responsible ear to the voice of his soul.

For this reason then, the analysand must and can find the healing or developmental forces within himself. Through the manifestations of the unconscious in the form of dreams, fantasies, images of various kinds, or in our case, through sand pictures, the analysand seeks contact with his Self, or put more simply, with the 'other' sides of his psyche (and his body), which have been repressed or forgotten or which never did have the power to emerge into consciousness. In the analytic situation he finds the free and protected space in which his consciousness can relax and in which can become effective the tendency of his soul toward self-regulation. The analyst cannot 'do it' for the analysand—that is, he cannot as if by proxy live this psychic process for him. Yet, he too experiences it 'with one joyful and one watchful eye'.

CHAPTER FOUR

The Imagination

With the sandplay method the analysand has an opportunity to let compensatory images enter, flow in, as it were, and then to shape them in the sand according to the power of his imagination. Through his 'Gestaltung' or design the images are formed, they are realized, and, because of the participation of the body, the emotions, and the soul, they become experience, images of experience. In my own work I have found that there are two roads leading from the unconscious psychic content to the formed, experienced sand picture and I shall describe these two roads here. One comes from the outside into the person. The other route leads from the inside to the outer picture.

When I say that the analysand has the opportunity to let the compensatory images 'enter' or 'flow in', as it were, I have chosen these words intentionally, because when I observe my analysands at the sand tray, I can often recognize this movement as a subtle flowing in, much like the flowing of a stream. At the beginning of an hour they sometimes sit there full of indecision, perplexed and wavering, or absorbed in themselves, saying that they have no idea what to do with the sand. Then we just wait quietly. When using the sandplay method, one does not need to 'do' anything; rather we try, if possible, to turn off and exclude this will and desire to act, our tense consciousness which always pressures us to achieve. On the contrary, we want to be relaxed, open, and receptive to that which enters and flows in. The precondition for this to happen is, of course, a room with a quiet, free, and protected atmosphere. (This atmosphere, incidentally, should also be free of the will and pressure of the analyst to achieve!)

Once such a receptive attitude is established, the hands of my analysands seem to pick up this current, move through the sand smoothly and leave behind traces much like the marks from a river. The formative process has now begun and slowly seeks its final form.

I should like to insist that it is incorrect to say that an analysand 'makes' the sand picture, rather he composes a picture or mediates an impulse which flows into him from the unconscious. He represents the movement of his soul in the sand at that particular time and place. The time and place of the analytic hour are decisive for what comes to pass. And because of this, Dora Kalff calls this the "free, and at the same time, protected space", because in it extraordinary psychic powers are constellated. Children, for instance, know for certain that during the therapy hour the entire therapy room and the therapist are there for them exclusively. This gives everything which happens during this hour special weight and promotes the process of self-development and self-healing of the child.

The current that enters the analysand is being nourished by those powers which, unconsciously, are active in him and which, in order to become conscious, must be formed and made recognizable. These energies are absorbed by the body, especially by the sensitiveness of the hands. We know from innumerable examples that the hands are extraordinarily sensitive organs. They can pick up energies and pass them on. They are the real mediators between the spiritual and material worlds. In the special case of sandplay, the inner mental picture is either being transformed by the hands into an external, concrete one which then not only can be seen but also touched. Or the transformation runs in the opposite direction. The hands take up the unconscious flow, make it visible and touchable in the sand, thereby calling forth an inner picture of process. In each case, however, the hands form the bridge between the psychic-mental world and material reality.

Some of the words in our language still retain the connection between the use of our hands and the importance of this expressive activity as a central meaning of our life. We speak of persons who are unable to 'handle' life or incapable of presenting their 'handiwork', who are unable to show, as it were, even if only metaphorically, the things that their hands have wrought. Such persons cannot make visible in the concrete world their inner powers and pictures and cannot, therefore, for this same reason, mediate them effectively to others. Although such persons might possess a rich interior world of pictures and experiences, it is their transformation and mediation into the external world by use of either their hands or language that is blocked. Since it is mostly fear which is at the root of such inability to act, it is extremely important that the analysand can practice and gain this experience in the mediating and transforming ability of his hands in the 'free and protected space' of the therapeutic atmosphere.

It is from this interaction of the mental and physical, the inner and the outer reality that the sand picture develops as a form of the imagination. The capacity for imagining and the power of the imagination is a specific and extraordinary ability of the human species. I would like therefore to discuss imagination somewhat in depth and will try to grasp its essence from various perspectives.

In C.G. Jung's 'Psychology and Alchemy' there is a significant citation concerning the essence of the imagination. Jung writes there about the psychic nature of the alchemical work, the opus, comprising the *theoria*, which forms the mental, philosophical part, and the *operatio*, which forms its practical, material execution. Jung quotes the alchemist Ruland as saying, "Imagination is the star in the man, the celestial or supercelestial body," commenting on his words as follows:

> This astounding definition throws a quite special light on the fantasy processes connected with the opus. We have to conceive of these processes not as the immaterial phantoms we readily take fantasy-pictures to be, but as something corporeal, a 'subtle body', semi-spiritual in nature. In an age when there was as yet no empirical psychology such a concretization was bound to be made, because everything unconscious, once it was activated, was projected into matter—that is to say, it approached people from outside. It was a hybrid phenomenon, as it were, half spiritual, half physical; a concretization such as we frequently encounter in the psychology of primitives. The imaginatio, or the act of imagining, was thus a physical activity that could be fitted into the cycle of material changes, that brought these about and was brought about by them in turn. In this way the alchemist related himself not only to the unconscious but directly to the very substance which he hoped to transform through the power of the imagination. The singular expression 'astrum' (star) is a Paracelsan term, which in this context means something like 'quintessence'. Imagination is therefore a concentrated extract of the life forces, both physical and psychic. So the demand that the artifex must have a sound physical constitution is quite intelligible, since he works with and through his own quintessence and is himself the indispensable condition of his own experiment. But, just because of this intermingling of the physical and psychic, it always remains an obscure point whether the ultimate transformations in the alchemical process are to be sought more in the material or more in the spiritual realm. Actually, however, the question is wrongly put: there was no 'either-or' for that age, but there did exist an intermediate realm between mind and matter, i.e., a psychic realm of subtle bodies whose characteristic it is to manifest themselves in a mental as well as a material form.[20]

This definition of the imagination as a "concentrated extract of the life forces, both physical and psychic" and the idea of an intermediate realm, a kind of subtle body between mind and matter are suitable when applied to sandplay as well. For me there is no question: not only during the times of the alchemists but today as well this intermediate realm between the psychic and the corporeal world still exists. I would simply not know how to define the phenomenon of sandplay otherwise. It arises out of the mind of the analysand and out of the psyche that dwells within matter. To put it more simply: out of the essence of the analysand and the essence of the sand and the figures there arises a new third. In this process the conscious as well as unconscious parts combine. A holistic fusion of the psyche and matter is experienced through the human body. For the person in whom this fusion occurs there results an experience which is indeed a union of what is conscious and unconscious, of body, soul and spirit and external matter. It is an experience which is connected to deep emotions and feelings. This experience touches the whole person and brings about a transformation or a maturation which does not have words and indeed, does not need words at that moment.

But, as I have already said, the outer composition of the sand picture is only its momentarily necessary form of appearance in the concrete world, yet in the final analysis it is not very important. The quintessence of the process at the sand tray is the inner picture which is full of the emotions and feeling of the creative process. And this should make clear that the idea of the 'sand picture' carries a double meaning: on the one hand, the concrete design in the sand tray; on the other, the inner picture which arises from it and which is charged with energy. This dual way of viewing a sand picture is most important for understanding the interpretation of sand pictures. We must look behind the external and static form of the picture and be aware of the symbolic meaning of the powers which have been set in motion and continue to move in the analysand.

In order that those readers who are not familiar with sandplay therapy can get a better feeling for this intermediate realm where the psychic and material elements meet and influence each other—indeed permeate and join with each other—I will describe in detail just how a sand picture comes into being.

Some analysands, in the days before the analytic hour, or even spontaneously at the beginning of their hour, form a more or less exact inner picture which they would like to create in the sand. Now one might think that it is easy to represent this inner picture concretely. Only persons who are very familiar with the nature of the medium in which they are about to work, that is the sand and the figures in our case, can imagine a picture in such a way that they can also make it. Their power of imagination is then, I would say, very well related to the medium. Most others will have difficulties in creating their images because both sand and the figures have a life of their own. Their images of the analysand are being transformed in the encounter with the unknown nature of the medium. Moreover, the hands of the analysands bring motifs and forms into the sand which are foreign to their consciousness. Where do these come from? From the unconscious of the analysands or from the sand?

Let us take the reverse route for a moment: The analysand sits at the beginning of the hour in front of the sand tray and does not know what he wants to do, but he waits quietly for that which will come to him. Suddenly, a current of inspiration will grip the analysand or the analysand experiences a rising and wholly unformed current in his body and begins to move his hands. A special feature here is that the body apparently has its own consciousness which is not connected with rational thinking, but rather with the imaginal world of the pictures. In this case we can say that the body knows more than the rational mind, and the impulse for the imagination arises from the body (on this see *Creation Myths* by Marie-Louise von Franz).

These flowing movements in the sand or the activity of just letting the sand run through one's fingers show that something has been set in motion in the analysand and his energy has begun to flow. For persons who are depressed and 'down' and who come cramped and lifeless to the analytic hour, these first signs of movement already mean quite a lot. At the beginning of treatment during the initial hours they might be the only expression in the sand. When the cramped state gives way to relaxation, it can happen that the shapes arising in the sand cause an association in the analysand or evoke an inner picture, which he then begins to form more elaborately. Now it may happen as in the previous case that during the process of playing in the sand, the sand behaves differently from what the analysand expected, or that the available figures are not suitable. Then the analysand is forced to modify his image considering the properties of the sand, or even to reject his original idea. If the wish or the will to model is present, he must learn to base his image upon the available medium and material, which means he must realize himself in relationship to the available reality and not force his idea upon it, or this would mean that the medium would be forced to participate: it would be raped. Another kind of nonrelatedness to the medium is present when the analysand—in the case where the sand doesn't behave in the way he wants it to—throws out the baby with the bathwater, as it were, rejecting both his inner picture and the disobedient sand and figures.

Even just the creation of the sand picture—the handling of the material along with experiencing one's own ability—promotes a certain development of consciousness. It is intensified by an exact inspection and grasping of the completed sand picture. Based on the slides which I take of completed sand pictures, follow-up is made possible and interpretive working through enhanced.

The lack of relatedness to the medium that I have mentioned can be illustrated quite aptly with the following example: adolescents will occasionally build a high mountain or tower in the sand, failing to take into consideration the properties of the material. They will pull the sand up ever taller and again and again the intended tower or mountain caves in. Finally, they become angry, hit the sand, and turn to another idea.

This is a mode of behavior which we can find not only in the therapeutic situation but also in everyday life in numerous variations. I'm thinking, for example, of a woman who wishes to sew a dress. She imagines a style and buys beautiful material for it. But already when cutting the material she has difficulties, and while sewing, the material keeps slipping away from the needle. The woman becomes angry, grows impatient and finally throws the material into a corner, 'because I'd never have an opportunity anyhow to wear such an unusual dress!'

Yet we not only deal in this way with outer things, but also do so occasionally with the inner: Someone intends from now on to write down his dreams daily in order to come to terms with them. But the dreams don't deliver the beautiful and imposing pictures and experiences which he had wished for and which would have justified the inconvenience of writing them down. So he throws the dream log into the corner, saying that 'preoccupation with one's own dreams is anyhow nothing but contemplating one's navel.'

Something similar also happens in human relationships. A young man—let's call him Fritz—gets angry with his colleague Franz because he is, from the point of view of Fritz, acting outrageously. Fritz didn't take the trouble to feel the 'why' of Franz's behavior, which would have given him the opportunity to understand the reasons for it. Fritz is behaving in just as egocentric and unrelated a manner toward Franz as the adolescent towards the sand, the seamstress toward her material and the dreamer toward his own dreams. They all accuse their 'other' of being the guilty party, regardless of whether this be a material, psychic or human kind, whereas the really guilty party is themselves, their own unrelatedness.

We can assume then, that the special therapeutic situation in sandplay will symbolize many different situations of everyday life and the analysand can learn here to interact with great care and empathy with something 'other', be it the sand or his own inner life.

This aspect of relatedness toward the other is most essential during sandplay. In every creative activity the person steps out of himself and into a relation to or with something other, sometimes a wholly unknown being. The creative work arises from the encounter between two elements and their connection. By virtue of this mutual action and reaction a continuous reciprocal effect comes into being, an exchange. Something new is generated which can be much more than the original components. In sandplay the new 'creature' is the sand picture which develops out of the interaction between the analysand and the sand with the figures. The precondition for the development of something new is, however, that the analysand really enters into the encounter with the unknown and unconscious in the sand and in himself and accepts the resulting challenge, lives through it and is creatively engaged in it. Being gripped emotionally during the creative activity effects his transformation. When later he takes . the inner picture with him, the imago of the sand picture, then it is full of the energies that were active at the time of composition. When we consider that the sand picture is the fruit of his activity, or metaphorically speaking, is the 'child' of the analysand, then we can understand that this 'child' is something extraordinary, in need of protection on the one hand and carrying great developmental energy, on the other.

The analyst, in such a situation, assumes not only the role of the midwife, but is also the witness of this 'birth', which is of vital importance. Psychically ill persons in whom we encourage a healing process through sandplay have great difficulty in accepting or even perceiving themselves. When the analyst notices and accepts the sand picture as a part of the analysand, he accepts thereby the analysand himself. Valuing both the analysand and the sand picture, the analyst teaches the analysand to meet the external and inner world with esteem as well. By example the analysand learns to take himself and 'the other' seriously and to recognize the meaning and importance of his own actions. Through the course of therapy he can develop a true religious attitude by increasingly encountering the inner and outer world carefully and conscientiously.

It goes without saying that a 'child'—something newly created—can arise not only from the encounter between the analysand and the sand but also from the encounter between the analyst and the analysand, from person to person. I don't mean, of course, a physical child but rather a 'relational child' or the pattern of relationship which is created out of the interaction between two persons. This mutually woven relational pattern is not visible or touchable as the sand picture is, but it exists and can even be perceived by a third person. This interactive pattern has an effect on the body and soul of the participants. This also can be seen as a form of imagination: a focal point or condensation of the energies of two persons, as a 'subtle body' in the intermediate world between the psyche and matter. Whether in the alchemical view, or during sandplay, or in the verbal analysis, the imagination is, as Jung says, "a concentrated extract of life forces, both physical and psychic."

When, during our therapeutic work, we wish to grasp the nature of the imagination more exactly, that's to say, when we wish to interpret it, we find that its meaning lies on different levels of consciousnesses. A sand picture usually can be seen to have an immediately recognizable meaning, but in the course of the passing days and weeks, while it makes its after-effects felt, there come deeper and yet more meaningful connections from the unconscious into consciousness. Each subsequent sand picture continues working on the previous one and contributes thereby to a meaningful transformation of the energies, leading toward the goal of healing the analysand or his reaching a higher level of consciousness.

To sum up my remarks, I would like to say that sandplay can achieve in a small space that which the person principally must do himself: transform and realize the unformed energies of his inner imaginative world into and through the concrete world, which is in our case sand. Once it has been concretely created, he must transform it again into an inner picture. This inner imaginative picture is now newly formed; it is a new creation because the originally unformed idea has been transformed both by virtue of the individual creative power of the person and of his relationship to the available, concrete world. In this way the analysand creates with his power of imagination through the sand picture his individual world and takes part, at the same time, macrocosmically in the continual great, creation of the world.

Now I would like to look at the nature of the imagination from another perspective. We also find the idea of the continual genesis of the world and the intermediate world of the imagination in the worldview of the Celts, and this idea I find very appropriate.

Celtic thought does not maintain a fundamental division between the psychic and the material world. In the Celtic conception, the psychic is the material and vice versa, both are forms of appearance and as such merely variants of the same energy. Matter is ultimately the realization of a thought, or really, the realization of the imagination.[21] (This view of the connection between psyche and matter is quite ancient and at the same time also new. Modern authors also—for example, the physicist, Fritjof Capra—have grappled with this complex of ideas.[22] From the point of view of analytical psychology both C.G. Jung and especially Marie-Louise von Franz have intensively written on this theme.[23]

The emphasis in the world of the Celts is on a state of consciousness of multiple significance and ambiguity, on the idea of a constant change of form, a continual creation. The cosmos is in motion with everything interlaced; the world is not just static but also in motion, becoming—in a veritable 'status nascendi'. There is available energy everywhere pressing toward creation. Generally speaking, we cling much too much to the assumed security of a static world. Everything that once has taken form, be it within or without, we seek to preserve. But life is vibration, constant movement and that is why we should learn not to think and live statically, but rather to learn to follow the movements and changes in life and participate in the continuously new creation of the world.

The Celts distinguish three worlds or three differing forms of appearance of the primordial energy:

> 1. The white world, the world of energy before the formation of the absolute, the world of the primordial images, the world of the archetypes. This world contains the creative potential of the not-yet-created. This world encompasses not only the origin and prefiguration of all that is created but also its goal. Time and space are suspended and the opposites are undivided.

> 2. The concrete world, the world of objects, the world of gross matter, the energy that has become form.

> 3. Between the world of the archetypes and the concrete world lies the world which the Celts called the watery world or the river world, the world of subtle-mattered energy, which is constantly in creative flux. In this world we find the landscape of the soul where the outer and inner are one, the world of the imagination and the subtle bodies of the alchemist.[24]

This intermediate realm of the imagination connects the world of the archetypes with the concrete world and it is possible to imagine it in the following manner: Through the power of the imagination we can transform the as yet unimaginable primordial images (because they are unformed energy) into a piece of concrete world creation. But we can also abstract, by virtue of the imagination, our experience and life events and contribute to the shaping of the primordial images. In this process of the transformation of energies by the imagination a decisive role is played by the morally responsible attitude of the individual. It is for this reason that the Celts did not think in terms of absolute Good or Evil. For them the vital thing was responsibility in action.

A short example can illustrate this point: take the case of the mother who is dominated by the negative, destructive aspect of the mother archetype; she can act out these powers unconsciously and poison the entire family. But when she feels that bad powers are at work in her, then she can in the course of sandplay therapy try to model these powers and thereby make them visible and recognizable. In the course of time she would continually gain new consciousness by modelling ever anew the modes of expression which these negative powers take in her and gain knowledge concerning the possibilities of how to avoid these negative effects upon her and her family—and perhaps even learn how to transform them into more positive ones. The necessary transformation of consciousness is decisively supported by paying attention to the unconscious components that show up in the sand picture or naturally also in the dreams following the sandplay. Again, the decisive element in the transformation of the woman is her honest readiness to confront herself and her taking careful and conscientious responsibility for her process.

In the sand pictures we can see and recognize especially well the world of the imagination which the Celts called the watery or the river world. By following a series of sand pictures we can trace this searching and flowing of energies and we can see how the energies are condensed and take form in order to continue to flow onward toward a new goal. One can trace this goal-oriented flow of energies beautifully in sand pictures by Maria (see Illustrations 32–39).

The Celtic view of the three worlds or the three differing modes of appearance of energy, is also related to sandplay. One can witness the mutual interconnection of these worlds during sandplay: the archetypes, seen as the universally human primordial images, constellate the freely flowing subtle energy. This energy is directed and intensified by human imagination. The imagination takes on concrete form in the sand picture again and again for a short time. It takes on body and then is taken back as an inner image into the inner-psychic world of the moved and moving imagination. The sand picture is itself a concrete form of energy but the inner picture provides a reserve of energy which can have spiritual, psychic, and bodily effects. The sand picture is most important, but only as a necessary intermediate stage. What is decisive is the process of transformation of the imaginative powers which arise from the recurring connection between the analysand and the sand, consciousness and the unconscious.

From the earlier example of the mother of a family we saw that negative aspects of a certain archetype can be constellated at the beginning of therapy. One can ask, now, whether negative archetypal powers can be constellated by the analyst which might have harmful or destructive effects upon the analysand? Or one can ask what the analyst can do so that positive, encouraging energies be constellated? These are absolutely fundamental questions, especially in nonverbal therapy where the unconscious channels between analyst and analysand are wide open. But to discuss these questions more extensively would go beyond the limits of this book.

The alchemical and the Celtic concepts of the essence of the imagination may interest readers who place greater emphasis upon the connections within the history of ideas. But there is also a discussion concerning the power of the imagination within the natural sciences. I refer here to the book *Imagery in Healing: Shamanism and Modern Medicine*, by Jeanne Achterberg, director of research and rehabilitation science at the University of Texas Health Science Center in Dallas. The title of this book expresses very well the two poles between which the author seeks for and establishes a connection.[25]

In the following I refer to those insights in Achterberg's book that seem to me important for an understanding of sandplay. I have discussed the different functions of the left and right hemispheres of the brain (above, pages 6–7). Here I wish to concentrate on the psycho-physiological aspects of imagery, or, in other words, physiological correlates of the image.

Achterberg takes for her point of departure the fact that images have both a direct and indirect effect upon physical reactions. The reverse is also possible. The image can result from participation of all sense organs, but can arise just as well without external stimuli such as light waves, sound waves, or odors. It is assumed that these images may trigger not necessarily identical but similar inner reactions to those evoked by the actual stimuli. For example, fearful images or intensely sexual fantasies are accompanied by dramatic physiological changes. States of physiological excitation are connected to images of injurious stimuli which are measurable by rate of heartbeat, muscle tone, and degree of skin contraction. (These measurable variables are also used in the so-called lie-detector and in analytical psychology in the association experiment.) Jeanne Achterberg infers from the pioneering work of various researchers that mental imagery is capable of controlling certain areas of the immune system.

In summing up the research on mental imagery and physiological process one can state the following:

(1) There is a connection between mental imagery and physiological processes.

(2) Mental imagery can either precede or follow physiological changes, a fact that points to both their causative and reactive roles.

(3) Mental imagery can be induced through conscious, intentional modes of behavior as well as through unconscious actions (electrical stimulation of the brain, dreams, dreamlike states, spontaneous creations such as sand pictures, and so forth).

Illustration 12

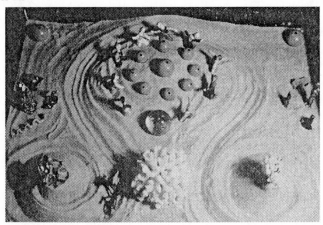

Sand Picture by a 42-year-old Woman. Uterus and ovaries are in a fertile, 'dancing' state.

Illustration 13

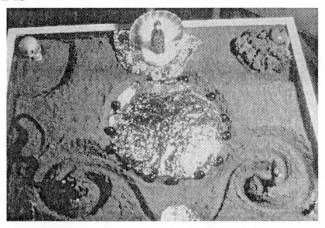

Sand Picture by a 38-year-old Woman. Uterus and ovaries between life and death.

(4) Mental imagery can be viewed as the hypothetical connecting link between the processing of conscious information and physiological change.

(5) Mental imagery can influence the peripheral as well as the vegetative nervous system.

Illustration 14

Sand Picture by a 45-year-old Woman. Left, the introverted, thinking side; right, the joyous, extraverted side; in the middle: the energetic connection.

During sandplay therapy we can observe the following physiological manifestations: The making of a sand picture can cause the analysand to experience very strong reactions such as shaking, perspiring, fainting, needing to urinate, crying; but also relaxation and calming of the heartbeat and breathing, release of tension in the stomach, a general improvement in sensory perception, and a feeling of happiness and wellbeing.

On the other hand a sand picture can also represent the condition of the body itself, for example, the 'happy' or 'sad' condition of the female sex organs (see Illustrations 12 and 13) or the personal unconscious representation of the left and right hemispheres of the brain (see Illustration 14). In Illustration 15 we can see the personal unconscious forming out of individual energy centers in the body. But in order to grasp the complete meaning of this sand picture we would have to know the life history of the analysand, her previous sand pictures and her own interpretation of this picture.

Images of the body, just like images in general, are the special domain of the right hemisphere of the brain. This right hemisphere is connected to the realm of the emotions and the vegetative nervous system. But the images are of a nonverbal or preverbal nature. If they are to be worked into meaningful thoughts they must be made available and intelligible to the left side of the brain. This is the reason why the clear and logical formulation of imagistic representations is so difficult and laborious.

Illustration 15

*Sand Picture by a 45-year-old Woman. Body
representation with visible energy centers,
the chakras.*

But on the other hand, the logical or interpretive discussion of
images is not even necessary in certain cases, if they affect the early,
elementary layers of human life in which the physiological and
psychological are to a large extent united. This is especially true in
child therapy where verbal interpretations are not necessary nor even
possible. We will learn from Maria's sand pictures how these deep
and primal layers in human life are represented and described
(below, pages 85–98).

The Symbolic Interpretation of Spatial Phenomena

A sand picture may embody several levels of consciousness simultaneously and, within these, various psychological states of a person. The meaning of a sand picture is as ambiguous and complex as the world of the person who creates it: after all, it is the spirit, psyche, and body, all of which play in the sand! Because it will be helpful to have available a general guide for the symbolic interpretation of spatial phenomena, I have prepared the following diagram based on generally valid criteria of picture interpretation and my own experiences with sandplay as therapy.

This diagram, however, is meant to be no more than an aid in orientation and we should, at all times, be willing to rethink general interpretative criteria and adapt them to the personal level of development of the analysand and his actual life situation.

With sandplay we face a special difficulty in that the spatial (three-dimensional) and surface-area (two-dimensional) qualities are intermixed and may be confused. Because we can work three-dimensionally with the sand, development in the sand tray is characterized from the bottom toward the top. Moreover, the analysand can either work downward into the bottom of the tray, or structures may rise upward out of the sand, as it were. On the other, he may work three-dimensionally with the sand or hardly touch it. Such differences must be considered when interpreting a sand picture. We must be mindful that if a person sculpts the sand, more light and shadow enter into his 'picture of the world'. Such a person is much closer to concrete, material reality and therefore his imagination has found much more of a created form.

We shouldn't forget that the analysand does not stand in the sand box, but in front of it. He therefore experiences the sand tray in a way similar to that in which he would a piece of paper on which he draws a picture. Thus, the rim of the sandbox closest to him is like the lower edge of the picture and the upper rim is like the upper edge of the picture. We principally interpret and photograph the sand picture from the point of view of its creator.

Guide for the Symbolic Interpretation of Spatial Phenomena

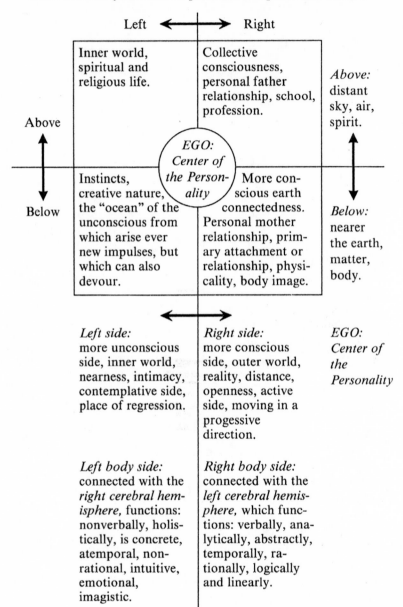

Left ←——|——→ Right

Inner world, spiritual and religious life.	Collective consciousness, personal father relationship, school, profession.
Instincts, creative nature, the "ocean" of the unconscious from which arise ever new impulses, but which can also devour.	More conscious earth connectedness. Personal mother relationship, primary attachment or relationship, physicality, body image.

EGO: Center of the Personality

Above ↕ Below

Above: distant sky, air, spirit.

Below: nearer the earth, matter, body.

←——→

Left side: more unconscious side, inner world, nearness, intimacy, contemplative side, place of regression.

Right side: more conscious side, outer world, reality, distance, openness, active side, moving in a progessive direction.

EGO: Center of the Personality

Left body side: connected with the *right cerebral hemisphere,* functions: nonverbally, holistically, is concrete, atemporal, non-rational, intuitive, emotional, imagistic.

Right body side: connected with the *left cerebral hemisphere,* which functions: verbally, analytically, abstractly, temporally, rationally, logically and linearly.

The center of the sand tray always contains the central motif. I have found that mandalas are invariably located in the centers of sand pictures. They do, after all, represent the various aspects of the relationship of the ego to the Self and, moreover, symbolize the centering of the personality.

Motifs which appear in the four corners of the sand tray provide a frame of reference for the unfolding of events. They represent the identifying, individual strands or components of the action.

Generally speaking, it has been my experience that new, spiritual impulses arise from the upper left corner (see Illustrations 19 and 41). Forces emerging from the lower left corner (see Illustrations 18, 33, and 41) point rather toward an increase of energies from the body and the instinctual spheres. Forces representing the outer world, such as the countertransference of the analyst onto the analysand may show up more from the right (see Illustrations 25 and 35). Leftward movements indicate regressions, or rather they indicate that energies may be flowing back into the unconscious. This may mean a going back—into the unconscious—or alternately a return to and collection of energies in the unconscious, intending a new goal, a new progression.

Movement from the lower left toward the upper right announce a development 'into life', into the external world, and can be seen frequently in the sand pictures of younger persons.

In more mature persons one often finds movement from the lower right toward the upper left. It points toward a development of the inner world of the spirit.

Eva: The Healing Process of a Severely Depressed Woman

Eva is an intelligent, very good-looking woman from a well-educated, upper-middle-class Swiss family. She is married and lives in a small village in Switzerland.

When she first contacted me she was 40 years old and had two school-age children. After high school graduation she did not enter college or complete any vocational training, but, since her marriage, she had held different part-time jobs. At the time when she began therapy with me, she was working in the helping professions and performed her job, objectively speaking, very well. Subjectively, however, she felt inadequate in her job, underestimated the value of her achievements, and often wanted to quit her job altogether. However, her colleagues and superiors persuaded her that her work was valuable, and this convinced her to continue working.

Eva had begun various therapies and analyses because of her deep depression and had actively participated in the therapeutic work. However, for various reasons, the therapies were always interrupted without producing visible improvement or healing. On the contrary, the problem of her unresolved tranference to her male therapists left additional deep wounds in Eva's confidence in herself as a woman. Her self-esteem fluctuated anyway despite her considerable beauty, health, and mental abilities; she sometimes felt a sense of moderate self-worth, but this was often followed by a deeply destructive self-hatred accompanied by massive feelings of guilt.

She expressed this self-hatred in two ways: she hit, scratched and cut her body, and she sought to destroy herself through both alcohol and misuse of medication. Alcohol and pills served primarily to cover up and repress the feelings of abandonment and anxiety which lay behind her self-hatred. These feelings sometimes reached such proportions that she only wished for peace and deliverance in the dissolution of consciousness or death. At such times she had herself hospitalized for several weeks so that she could find rest and protection. The secure atmosphere of the clinic was good for her for a short time, and the medication reduced her anxiety and suicidal feelings.

Hospitalization did not change Eva's psychic condition. In my opinion, no change could have occurred during those few weeks, even with the best possible care. But fortunately, these weeks made it possible for Eva to survive.

To sum up, one could say that Eva suffered from a deep narcissistic disturbance.

For reasons of discretion I can say little concerning Eva's youth and family relationships. She was an only child. Her mother had a depressive personality structure. Her mother's confidence in herself as a woman and in life as such was disturbed by a very deep traumatic experience, so that she couldn't give to her daughter a positive attitude toward herself and the world. Rather, Eva experienced feelings of abandonment, inferiority, and anxiety.

Eva's father was an achievement-oriented, rational man. Eva had a positive relationship to him and he to her, but this mutual affection did not prove sufficient to enhance Eva's feelings of self-worth. Her father was unable or unwilling to understand the causes of his daughter's continuing deep depressions, nor could he empathize with them. He believed that willpower makes everything possible; a depression should yield to an effort of the will, and hard work, or at least be held in check.

Eva's husband's attitude was similar to her father's. He had trouble understanding that his wife's illness was not the result of being spoiled, ill-willed, or malicious, but the result of a wound at the foundation of her existence, a wound which was continuously being torn open. He believed that conscious will and discipline could bring some order into his wife's life. Neither he nor her father could empathize with Eva's abysmal sense of abandonment and fears.

I cannot further elaborate on the reasons for all this. But I want to point out that today it seems that a man in a leading position must repress fears and feelings of weakness and abandonment. To admit to such feelings would naturally weaken the level of performance which is demanded of him. It is not too far-fetched to think that these repressed, dark sides of the soul are shoved onto the 'weaker' family members, such as the wife and the daughter, and they must live them, as it were, by proxy.

The 'will' which is so emphasized by both men is defined in analytical psychology as "that psychic energy which is freely available to consciousness". If we think about this definition we can see that a person cannot mobilize his will and use it for focussed action when he or she suffers from such fundamental abandonment and self-alienation as Eva. She needed all her energy just to survive, and as we shall see later from her sand pictures, it looked as though she was bleeding to death. Her life energy was being drained and no replenishing inner source had yet developed (see Illustration 24).

This lack of understanding of suffering that is not rationally comprehensible is very common today. This suffering is often so deeply repressed that the person himself is no longer able to feel it. It is a commonly held view in our achievement-oriented society that the psyche can be directed by reason alone and that healing of psychological troubles could be brought about if only the patient 'wanted' to be well. The delicate and vulnerable nature of the psyche is simply ignored and time and space, which are necessary for development, are not provided. The needs and expressions of the psyche are largely repressed and achievement, development, progress, stability and order take their place.

Especially in the masculine world there are many verifiable and convincing reasons for repressing the soul and calling psychological suffering the expression of a weak-willed, ineffective personality. Nonetheless, the suffering persists. Any person will suffer when he cannot accept his own life positively. Women especially experience much pain and distress because of the restrictions and limits placed upon their freedom of self-expression. I chose the name "Eva" intentionally, because many other women suffer for the same reason, although perhaps not in such great measure.

Eva had heard about me in connection with sandplay. On her first visit to my office I saw that she was very sad, pale, and cramped. Her body was tightly drawn together and she seemed rigid and cold, as if all energy and warmth had withdrawn to a deep interior place. While sitting she often assumed a fetal position. She crossed her arms in front of her, as if she wished to protect her heart. She cried a lot and told me about her life in an unconnected way. She repeatedly expressed no hope of improvement and insisted that she was unable to trust anyone. In order to go back to sleep in the morning she took alcohol and pills. In this way she neglected her family and her work, which once again made her feel inferior and guilty.

Eva looked like a half-dead, frozen bird and my natural impulse would have been to take her into my arms to warm her. I didn't do it because half-frozen creatures have to be warmed up very carefully. But because analysts are humans too, I made her a cup of coffee, indicating without words, that I sensed how cold she might feel in her heart. The first encounter with an analysand is very important for me. My 'eye' is then not yet clouded by any conscious knowledge. During this hour—as in most hours—I said very little and simply listened. I tried instinctively and intuitively to grasp what kind of a human being might be hidden behind this sad, frozen woman.

One detail from the earliest meetings seems to me important to mention: as is often the case of analysands with a strong disturbance in their feelings of self-worth, Eva could never say whether she would come for another hour of therapy. She did not believe in the possiblity of improvement, that is, her lack of confidence in life prevented her from having any hope. Without debating the ins and outs of this, I explained to her that improvement was possible only if she would give herself, her unconscious, and me the necessary time so that she could develop. At the second meeting I therefore suggested that she commit herself again, without any ifs and buts, to at least ten more hours of therapy. I was able to take this decisive position because, I had already seen her first sand picture (Illustration 16). This proved to be helpful. Eva said later that this had been the decisive push for our long analytic work together.

During the second hour Eva arrived similarly pale and cramped but it did not seem to me that she had come unwillingly. During the course of the hour she went to the sand tray. In my office I have one tray with light, usually dry sand and a second tray with a somewhat darker, very fine beach sand. Eva chose the darker, earthier sand and moistened it with water. Obviously, she did not experience any fears or blocks concerning the earthy, physical quality of this moist sand. On the contrary, she seemed to seek out this more solid, moldable material. Then, hesitatingly and tearfully, she formed her first sand picture.

Eva's First Sand Picture

Although Eva seemed sad and cramped, dissolved in tears and disoriented, her hands worked the sand quietly, delicately, and with increasing certainty. To my great astonishment and with growing emotion, I watched the making of her first picture: it was centered and balanced, a beautiful and confident picture of order! To understand why I was so touched by her sand picture, one has only to recall Eva's history. Here was a woman who had been severely depressed for years, who depended on various medicines and hospitalization, and who had come to me without any hope of ever getting better.

Now she had created a circular, three-layered, primordial hill, perfectly structured in four parts. This round hill was framed by a circle which protected and contained it. The protective circle was firmly anchored in the corners of the sand tray.

Illustration 16

This picture represents a three-dimensional mandala. The San-skrit word mandala means circle, a meaningful circle. Mandalas in the form of circular structures can also be found in nature, in diverse human representations, and in spontaneous manifestations of the psyche. They express totality, comprehensive wholeness, and an image of the divine. Mandalas, sometimes structured in four or more parts, can be a symbol for the cosmos, the creator-God, the omnipresent creative energy, the seasons of life, or the succession of the four seasons of the year. Viewed psychologically, mandalas represent psychic wholeness, the archetype of the Self. As we shall see from Maria's sand pictures (Chapter 7 below), circular forms on which certain figures are placed represent concrete aspects of specific archetypes. These are, in turn, partial aspects of the wholeness of the Self. Jung speaks of the archetype of the Self as representing the principle of wholeness and order, and as a psychic process of centering.[26] He also speaks of mandalas that appear spontaneously in dreams and imagination and of the unconscious attempt of the psyche to center and heal itself.[27] The mandala represents a scheme of order contained in a protective circle superimposed over psychic chaos and the tendency toward dissolution (a tendency the psyche does indeed have).

In Eva's sand picture the mandala was a spontaneous expression of her psyche to try to protect and center her. I felt this reaction of her unconscious to her disoriented condition as favorable for her therapy. I took the solid anchoring of the protective circle in all four corners of the sand tray to be Eva's unconscious longing for protection and support which, viewed from a larger perspective, corresponds to the wish for the 'free and protected space' of the therapeutic setting.

It seems to me important to include a few relevant remarks concerning the course of Eva's therapy. She came regularly once or twice a week. During the first 20 months she was very sad, despairing, and unstable, partly due to her misuse of alcohol and medication. She wept a lot during the therapy hours but also told me quite a bit about her life. During this period she created a sand picture every week. She worked mostly in silence at the sand tray, and afterwards said little. But almost always at the end of the hour Eva seemed calm and more relaxed. Sometimes she seemed almost a little happy with her sand pictures. Between therapy hours, during her dark and depressed moments, she would also call me at home. During these phone calls and during other times of despair and sadness at the sand tray, I always tried to show that I could feel what she felt and that I took her suffering seriously. But I also attempted to keep her very close to ordinary reality, to help orient her in time and place and guide her to take appropriate action when possible.

When she was dissolved in tears in the therapy sessions, I would put my arm around her shoulder or hold her hand in order to give her some human warmth, and in order to keep her in the here and now through body contact. I believe that physical contact in therapy is important and helpful but the analyst should not awaken wishes or hopes of a sort which he cannot or will not fulfill. I acted on the principle that 'like produces like', that is that the calm hand of the analyst can create calmness in the analysand.

I did not try to address the cause of Eva's depression because she would not yet have been able to bear this. Similarly, I avoided encouraging or comforting her verbally or expressing my delight with and admiration of her very impressive sand pictures. It seemed that she sank ever more deeply into her depression with every heightening of her self-esteem. I was able to mention her creative talents only cautiously, because she is a very talented woman. But again, such an insight would flood her with sadness and guilt. After all, it was her contention that she was unable to live out her talents.

After I had seen Eva's first sand picture as her psyche's attempt to center and heal herself, I tried during the first 20 months of therapy to support Eva in her external life, to keep her going, figuratively speaking, 'on a backburner or a small flame', to gain time for her unconscious, psychic process to unfold. And of course, thanks to the sand pictures we were able to share in this process. Metaphorically speaking, Eva's shakily constructed house of the soul, about to fall apart, needed a strong and stable foundation, upon which a new house could be built. This is not to say that the foundation work would be built from the outside, by the analyst. It had to be created from within Eva's unconscious psyche. As Eva's analyst, I was simply a construction foreman. It was my job to see that the specifications coming from Eva's inner master builder were correctly followed.

Only when the rooms in the new house were ready for habitation, could the old, weak house be torn down. While the foundation was being built there was enough energy only to keep the old house from collapsing, but not yet enough for constructing the new building. Eva's sand pictures gave me hope that she could be cured, even though months would pass before she would participate visibly in her sand pictures. As the therapy progressed my hopes were strengthened because I could see how, albeit slowly, in Eva's unconscious the necessary archetypal images were being construct-ed. From them she could gradually gain the energy to heal her early and deep wound. I should say that Eva's pictures meant a lot to me. Without them I wonder if I could have marshalled the strength and patience to carry on this extraordinarily difficult therapy. We need to remember that an analyst is not an inexhaustible fountain. Often one needs to give more than it is possible to draw from within at a particular moment. During such moments, viewing a picture or listening to music can nourish a person, so certain sand pictures of my analysands become a source of strength to me.

The 16 sand pictures I shall now consider are a selection from the many which Eva created during a 20-month period. I view them retrospectively and will try to interpret them in such a way that the features both of their extraordinarily creative designs and of their emotional power are not destroyed. We should not forget that we must put up with a certain amount of intellectual explication in order to grasp the underlying sense of these pictures. Nonetheless, the essential point about them is experiencing them and being gripped and stirred while viewing them!

Let us return once again to the first picture. We notice the three layers of the hill. In hindsight, from the successive therapeutic sessions, we can view these three layers as prefiguring the threefold division of a person into body, soul, spirit, or, the earth as the material world, the subtle, psychic world, and the spiritual world of the absolute, the archetypes. This would also represent the totality of the creative energy in its three aspects: energy before being formed, energy in motion searching for form and energy which has become form.

The cross over the hill can be seen as Eva's unconscious attempt to orient herself. If we imagine that we are standing on a hill and we can see the horizon as an infinite circle around us, and the earth at our feet as an unlimited, unordered plane, it is possible for us—because of the course of the sun—to orient ourselves according to the four cardinal points. Then we are standing as human beings in the center of the world, in the center of the cross with the four arms forming the four cardinal points. In this way we have created the possiblity of orientating ourselves as we turn away from the chaos of unlimited and unordered nature.

We can view the sand picture from yet another point of view. The circular form of the hill reminds us of a funeral mound or the maternal womb. If we recall that the sand tray, like the alchemical vessel of alchemy, is a kind of uterus, that is, a maternal womb in which the psychic substance is being cleansed and transformed in order to be reborn in a new form, then we may see the hill as a place of death and rebirth, doubly protected by the circle and the sand tray.

Eva's Second Sand Picture

Illustration 17

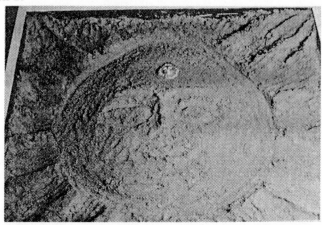

Where the primordial hill had been located in the previous sand picture, Eva now formed a large sun which again filled the entire space of the sand tray. Next, she placed a small golden sun in the spot of the forehead-chakra, commonly referred to as the 'third eye', as if she wished to say, 'The small sun recognizes the larger sun', or 'I, a human being recognize you, God.'

The sun is our source of light and warmth and represents our life energy. 'The sun brings all things to the light,' says a German proverb, and this means that the sun makes all things discernible. The sun is a symbol for illumination, cognition, and consciousness. The sun does not change form, but appears every morning on the horizon in the very same round wholeness. With the naked eye we cannot recognize the true shape of the sun, but we do experience its effects constantly. So the sun is a symbol for the everlasting and unchangeable, for God, and for the nature of the archetypes which in their wholeness can never be fully grasped, but whose energetic effects are felt again and again.

Plato likened the sun to the Ideas. The Ideas (eidos) represented for him that which is unchangeable, the form behind each thing, its true being. In this way the sun symbolizes simultaneously the power and the effect which emanate from one's true being. This power and the effect from within, our personal sun as archetype, as it were, can be felt.

The idea of human wholeness, the body, soul, and spirit, is referred to as the archetype of the Self in analytical psychology. The Self has an ordering power which directs the development of the person so that we could call it the higher personality, comprising both conscious and unconscious aspects. It directs development insofar as this power becomes effective within a person.

Many persons live in conscious connection with their Self. The Self with its ordering power becomes the guide on the road toward individuation. Many persons unconsciously have a good relationship to their Self, which, in that case, stands much like a guardian angel behind them.

But others, especially those who, like Eva, have experienced early narcissistic wounding cannot find their connection to their wholeness and its ordering, guiding power. Their Self is overshadowed. Kathrin Asper describes this in her book *Abandonment and Self-Alienation*:

> Since he is not related to his inner being, the narcissistically wounded person cannot look inward because of the dark and destructive contents that are in his inner life. Because of this, the chances of connection to his own Self are continually being frustrated and this darkness inside is perpetuated. The goal of transformation in a person suffering from the problem of narcissistic self-alienation can be reached by establishing both a positive, loving relationship to oneself and a more tolerant attitude toward others. Actually, this is a process in which the person's full potentialities that had up to then been overshadowed and crippled, reach the light. It is useful to recall here the many heroines of fairy tales who in the end emerge from a life in humiliation and darkness dressed in luminous clothes adorned with ornaments representing the sun, the moon, and the stars . . .[28]

Still unknown to Eva's consciousness, her hands had their own awareness, as we see in this picture where her Self steps into the light. It is an extremely important event reinforced, moreover, by the sun in the 'third eye', which makes human beings clairvoyant and enables the soul to differentiate the divine light in all of its forms of appearance. An old commentary on the third eye describes it as follows:

> The soul casts a glance at the form of the spirit. A ray of light issues forth, dispelling the darkness. Distortions, ill and wrong forms die and all small fires expire. Lesser lights can no longer be seen. Through the light the eye awakens the necessary forms of being. This brings knowledge to the adept. An ignorant person will not discover any meaning.[29]

Because Eva was not able at that time to look inward consciously, her hands gave form to her unconscious knowledge, in the sand. Evidently, during that hour, as the old text would suggest, Eva's soul cast a glance at the Self. A ray of light issued forth and the darkness disappeared. The picture of her Self became light like a sun. This lighting up of the Self in the depth of her unconscious soul did not really become visible in her everyday life for some time to come; nonetheless, the effect was reflected in the next pictures.

Eva's Third Sand Picture

Illustration 18

This picture radiates the concentrated solidity, security, and strength of the earth. The square earthen house is in itself both a symbol for the earth and a temple for the earth-mother. Originally, the house was covered with a roof made of moss and tree bark. I opened it, so that the lady of the house, its proprietress, the dark, earthy mother with her child can be seen. The house is protected by a circle of blue pebbles, which represent water, and is embedded in verdant nature. The plant world and water, springs next to or underneath her sanctuaries, all belong to the earth-mother.

From the lower left side, also from the realm of the earth, a dark-skinned figure brings bread. This bread is the gift of the earth-mother. The sand picture speaks not of an 'Our Father', whom we customarily address in our prayers, as in the well-known Lord's Prayer, but in a most beautiful way it gives utterance to an 'Our Mother'. Here, 'our mother, who art on earth', gives the daily bread, the basic food of our body.

Over the gate to the earth house is placed again, much like the 'third eye', the round picture of a small child. "The soul casts a glance at the form of the spirit," is stated in the commentary on the third eye. Because of this picture we can see that Eva's soul cast a glance at the primordial image of the life-giving, protecting, and nourishing mother in the forms of plants, earth, water, house, body, and woman. This perfectly centered picture radiates the natural, deep peace and calm and the feeling of acceptance which a child experiences on the lap of a loving mother or which anyone can experience when embraced by great mother nature. Eva did not sufficiently experience this primal feeling in her childhood, but now, in the protected space of the analytical situation, the appropriate and corresponding energy potential could be constellated. It is evident that the field of energy belonging to the positive aspect of the mother archetype is not solely restricted to the physical mother but comprises the earth, nourishing nature, the warming and protecting house, life-giving water, and much more.

During analysis, the comprehensive experience of the good mother earth forms the foundation for constructing the house of the soul. We know that a stable house cannot be built unless it is on a solid foundation!

Eva's Fourth Sand Picture

After the circle of the radiant sun and the square of shaped earth, we see a moving, flowing, iridescent picture. The center is formed by a recumbent lunar crescent covered with shiny gold thread. Water flows around this from a spring in the form of a heart, Eva said. Or is it, perhaps, after all, a veil, a subtle-bodied fluid, corresponding to the material from which Eva fashioned this river of water? The mistress who is the owner of this picture is a feminine figure whose

Illustration 19

dark blue mantle is dotted with stars. Her position is emphasized
with the addition of seashells and a white coral, which forms a wreath
of light.

I had myself made this 'Queen of the Night' or 'Lady of the Stars'
figure a long time ago, as a counter piece to the earth-mother. I felt
that for sandplay therapy, I needed a figure to express those qualities
of the soul and spirit in motherhood which contrast with its earthy,
instinctual aspects. But she has become much more than this: a
cosmic figure, the queen of heaven, Lady Moon, the world soul,
opaque and veiled, unfathomably fascinating. Much like the starry
night sky and the moon, she can draw the person into another sphere.
This experience may be inspiring and expand consciousness, but it
may also bring about dissolution of consciousness and destruction.

The constituting elements present the condensed primordial
picture of the feminine soul: the moon, fascinating, moving, and ever
changing; the water or veil, flowing and moving; the heart; the
mussels; and the dark, yet radiant stellar Lady with her starry coat.
She truly is not, but rather she flows and changes constantly. She is
not immutable and radiant like the sun, nor does she have the solid
forms of earth, but is nocturnal, soft, unfathomable, mysterious, and
secretive. As lovely as this picture is, it is hard to explain, even
unfathomable. Without the brightness, the illumination from the sun
and the solidity of the earth, it may portend the dangers which the
moon and the watery world hold in store: insanity or the dissolution
of the psyche, which in a manner Eva had experienced in her darkest
moments of depression.

Eva made these three pictures one after another in a very short
time. They represent the three archetypal fields of energy: the

spiritual, the physical, and the psychological, all three of which act and react on one another and form a wholeness. For Eva, they had a positive effect. But we should not forget that each image has negative aspects as well: the sun as one-sided, excessively bright consciousness can dry up and scorch a person. It can distance one from the reality of the earthly body. The earth, the body, can trap people in the weight and immobility of their forms. The watery, flowing lunar world of the soul, which is also the world of the imagination, may lead to one's dissolution in the infinity of the unformed world.

Eva's Fifth Sand Picture

Illustration 20

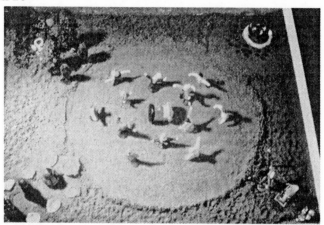

This picture shows a round center, but the action is essentially determined by the powers coming from the four corners of the sand tray. In the center the sun and the moon face each other; between them is a crystal. Six female figures dance in an inner circle while six masculine figures dance in an outer circle. The moon is located center left; that is the side of feeling and imaginative ability. In addition, feminine energies rise from the lower left: the Lady of the Stars, earth-mother and a round, peasant-like mother-figure. She brings a vessel probably containing a gift of earthly nourishment. On either side of these figures are shells opened toward the sky as if they were receiving hands, which contain spiritual food. The sun is at the right, the side connected with the intellect and logical thinking. From the lower right (poorly visible), masculine energies emerge: a Buddha image, a wise man and a shaman bring two swords. These do not represent war or fighting, but rather the weapons of the spirit, of knowledge, and of culture.

In this picture we can most clearly see a meeting of the 'higher opposites': moon and sun, nature and culture, the feminine (nourishing primordial energy), and masculine (technology). They meet for a grand union of opposites the alchemists called Thio, the 'conjunctio oppositorum'.

Is it not impressive to watch the dynamics unfolding in this meeting of opposites? What joy and movement the dancing figures express!

Through the play of opposites in the dance something new emerges: the crystal. This crystal corresponds to the 'stone', the 'lapis' of the alchemical process, the 'treasure hard to attain', the Self. The alchemists said that the lapis consisted of body, psyche, and spirit and was a living being. We can agree with this even today, for the lapis or crystal is a symbol of wholeness of the inner, higher personality.[30]

Eva's Sixth Sand Picture

Illustration 21

This impressive picture presents the union of opposites of our Christian image of God standing at high elevation: The crucified Christ and the human being belong together. They are suspended between heaven and earth, between above and below, right and left, with a tension which can only arise from such symbols of opposites.

This is bearable only by focussing inward to one's own ordering center, or outward to the image of God. From this perspective, Christ became the centering and healing figure, one which could confront the negative, dissociating sides of Eva's psyche.

Summary

These six unconsciously-formed pictures show the first steps of Eva's inner process. Apparently, the intensive energies of the archetypes had to come first to strengthen Eva so she could confront her suffering and her inner problems. These archetypal images have a strong effect even on the uninvolved viewer. They must have gripped Eva all the more strongly. From the depth of her unconscious psyche, Eva received energies that enabled her to begin to think about consciously confronting her psychic suffering.

The following picture introduced a nine-month-long series of emotionally upsetting pictures, which expressed Eva's feelings of utter abandonment. They show her pain and represent her threatening fear of death. By repeatedly expressing her problems in the sand and making them thereby visible, counterforces of healing emerged. We hardly spoke during this time. When we did speak it was to talk indirectly about the sand pictures. I tried in a warm, but careful way to help Eva survive from day to day, but placed the main emphasis on the process in the sand tray.

Eva's Seventh Sand Picture

With the healing image of Christ before her inner eye, Eva could now begin the confrontation with her personal opposites.

A crescent moon is visible in a round lake. To the right stand death and the devil. Spiders and horrible vermin crawl about, representing her inner fears. She lived very near to this dark side which dominated her life.

To the left is the good earth-mother. On the third step of the entrance to a temple sits the Buddha image, a symbol for positive spirituality.

The central motif of the crescent moon represents the nature of Eva's problem. Under the cross we can see her own grave. She explained that the little child embodied her soul between a light and a dark angel, the powers of good and evil. Eva thought this picture

Illustration 22

expressed sadness and great despair, but I saw that it contained elements of hope. First, the moon was waxing brighter and more full of life. I noticed a white fish in the center and a little ship pointed toward the left, the positive side. Fishes are fruits of the sea, an old symbol of fertility. The fish is also a manifestation of the soul; in this picture it points to something light and good.

At the end of this therapy session, I cautiously assured Eva that there were signs of hope in this picture. But at that time she could not yet go into this. I think that my carefully phrased remark had a positive effect.

Illustration 23

Eva's Eighth Sand Picture

A sharp division into two halves is unmistakable in this picture. The colorful and bright external world is on the right. Eva cowers miserably to the left in the grip of the red and the green demons. She called one "envy" and the other "hate". From the upper left a black snake threatens her and from the lower left, death. They make her apprehensive. She would like to move across into the colorful world, but the black angel of death stands at the gateway and turns her back. He says that she has no right to this joyous colorful world, that she belongs to the realm of anxiety and death. The skull and the black snake may indeed be frightening; however, both may also function as symbols of transformation and rebirth.[31]

I carefully explained to Eva that her entire sand picture formed an image of her psyche and that it contained a happy side. Eva took note of this remark.

What is extraordinary about sandplay is that an analysand, even if he were mostly unconscious while making his picture, cannot overlook what he has made. He has placed positive and negative elements into the sand. He is responsible for them. He mirrors himself in the sand tray. It is also true, of course, that 'seeing the mirror images of one's psyche' is not the same as recognizing and knowing oneself. But in the course of analytical work, step by step new parts of the psyche appear; that is they are made conscious until a composite image of the soul is recognizable.

Illustration 24

Eva's Ninth Sand Picture

Here we can see another round hill within a protected circle. Eva lies in the center, nailed to the earth. A figure backs away from her. This figure had stabbed her with a dagger in the stomach, creating a gaping, bloody wound. Vast amounts of blood flow from this wound. But standing behind Eva and protecting her is the Queen of Heaven, in front of a greening cross.

At first this picture evokes immense pain, suffering, and compassion. One feels it in both the heart and the stomach. The flow of blood from the center of feminine life reminds us of menstruation and miscarriage or perhaps a severe injury in the center of the feminine psyche. In Swedish, the maternal womb (uterus) is also called the 'livmoder', or the mother of life. Naming the specific organ in this way suggests the essence of that greater nature 'which brings forth life'. The area of the psyche we call the creative unconscious belongs here, not just one's relationship to one's mother. This is where Eva had been deeply injured. The retreating figure embodies all those experiences and all those persons who had caused this wound.

Here I would like to ask my readers to reflect on the places where they daily harm the 'mother of life' and how they do it, both materially and psychically.

If we recall Eva's first sand picture which contained the archetypal hill, or maternal womb, we can now see that this womb has been opened to release its suffering. If we look more closely, however, we can see that within the inner circle, there is a lunar crescent. As Eva stated, "the moon has become one with the sun." Also, the Queen of Heaven stands in front of the place where the cross is sprouting, indicating that this is a place of suffering but also of healing.

These three pictures give us a glimpse of the many pictures which Eva created over the next nine months. They were pictures of suffering, of psychic death and anxiety due to her feelings of guilt. The grave, the skull, the angel of death, being crucified and bleeding as if suffering from an immense menstruation, all these are symbolic representations of the psychological condition a person experiences when he faces the darkness, when he has descended to the realm of the shadows, and experiences the death of his existing conscious attitude. In many sand pictures Eva depicted herself as having been torn to pieces. The motif of dismemberment of the existing personality and its decay is a widely disseminated motif in mythology, fairytales, and initiation rites.[32]

In the alchemical process, dismemberment, death, and the decay of the psychological structure of the personality is called *nigredo—*

the darkening or blackening. It is also called *mortificatio*, the killing.
What is meant by *nigredo* is an encounter with the night, with the
darkness of the personal or collective unconscious. Through such
an encounter the ego and its conscious attitude is so radically shaken
and dissolved that it suffers a psychic death. But at the darkest
moment, when one is at one's wits' end, at the moment of complete
helplessness and despair, there emerges a new light in the soul, just
as we experience it seasonally at Christmas, or at the winter solstice.
We experience these events both within and without. After the
'nigredo' there is the 'albedo'—the dawn, the whitening, which
corresponds to spring. Then follows the *rubedo*, or the reddening,
the time of sunrise, or summertime. These terms signify that after
the ego is dissolved, and the person experiences his psychological
death, a new level of consciousness, a brighter, broadened way of
being is formed.

It should be clear from this discussion that both the analysand and
the analyst experience the nigredo as a most difficult time. It is a time
when images of death arise, when death-wishes and suicidal thoughts
surface. Such a passage through the darkness should in no way be
mitigated or avoided because of fear or weakness of the analyst! A
confrontation with the skull, the contemplation of death and
eternity, seem to be the preconditions for a true transformation.
Jung states that a renewal of consciousness is possible only after
experiencing death.[33]

For Eva, the time of the *nigredo* was easier to bear because
she was able to work out her problems both literally and figuratively, piece by piece, in the sand. Psychic contents which had
been unknown to her up to that time became visible. Her negative side, for example, her envy and hatred, presented great
challenges to her. But the central point of her *nigredo* was this: she
had to learn to bear and accept her own tendencies toward darkness, toward dissolution, including her death-wishes, without suc-
cumbing to them. And even if the persons near her rejected and
condemned this side in her, it was imperative that she learn to live
with it, as she was one of those for whom death and darkness are
constant companions.

Eva's Tenth Sand Picture

This picture was created approximately four weeks after the last one.
We can see a caravan loaded up with goods. The leader guides the
caravan into the center of a spiral. In the lower left corner lies Eva

Illustration 25

as a small child, enclosed in a circle of stones. Her umbilical cord extends all the way over to the lower right where the parents are tied together. However they are separated from the rest of the sand picture by a glass wall and the umbilical cord is broken. Thus, the child no longer has any connection to the parents but is abandoned and isolated. This is how Eva saw her conscious condition, but the unconscious central motif says something different.

Symbolically the spiral is related to the labyrinth. Particularly during initiations, one enters into and departs from the spiral, movements signifying symbolic death and rebirth. For example, the initiate enters the body of the earth-mother to die there and to be reborn. That is why the spiral can also serve as a symbol for the uterus.[34] In sandplay, one often encounters a spiral with a definite entrance and exit. It represents the female sexual organs and can express fertilization, pregnancy, or birth.

This picture shows that nourishing energies bring fertilization in the depths of the unconscious. This is an important, promising event and is in contrast to Eva's conscious feeling of abandonment by her parents.

When Eva made this picture, she had been in therapy with me for a year. It had been a difficult year not only for Eva but for me as well. Perhaps we could compare it to the difficulties a caravan leader encounters when passing through a desert. What is required of him, one might ask? Perhaps the same qualities as those needed by an analyst: to know the way and to persevere without losing nerve or becoming despondent. It seems to me that the positive effects of the therapeutic attitude are mirrored in this sand picture.

Eva's Eleventh Sand Picture

Illustration 26

This picture shows a green world, cheerful and full of life, but it is split in two by the "great wound", as Eva called it. This wound looks like a stone grave on which a snake is resting.

We know about Eva's wound from her life history and her pictures. Lacking basic self-confidence and trust in life, she suffered and grieved because as a woman she felt inferior, despised and misunderstood by everyone. But now the wound has closed; it is no longer open and exposed. The snake, an ancient symbol of nature's healing power, has helped the wound to close and cicatrize. At the very end of the hour Eva consciously placed a path across the wound as a sign that it was bridgeable.

The next four pictures followed in four- to five-week intervals.

Eva's Twelfth Sand Picture

This picture is divided into an upper and a lower part, symbolizing respectively the external world and Eva's inner world. From below, out of the earth and the physical realm we can see the rising flames of a huge fire. It is the fire of the emotions, in which Eva, once again nailed down (as in Illustration 24), lies suffering in isolation from the external world. The flames are the fires of hell. On the left we can see a red devil. Eva said that the devil is delighted by her suffering. The people in the external world turn their backs on Eva's torment. She

Illustration 27

is alone with herself. Or alone with God, since a large god-image
watches over the events from the lower edge of the tray.

It is a frightening and deeply moving picture. Eva is suffering the
pains of purgatory. Here is the lonely torment of a woman wrestling
with a far-reaching transformation of her personality: an expansion
of consciousness and a renewal of her relationship with her Self and
her god-image.

Fire means burning emotion and inner heat, suffering and pain.
But it also signifies cleansing and transformation. Eva was cleansing
herself from her death-wishes, her despair and feelings of inferiority,
her envy and hate. This intense fight was over who would prevail: her
negatively-charged and weak ego, or a stronger, more stable ego
capable of finding a new relationship to the ordering, constructive
and life-enhancing aspects of her psyche.

This fiery and far-reaching process of transformation within a
course of therapy is most painful and difficult for both analysand
and analyst. The analyst accompanies and strengthens the analysand
sharing in her suffering to some extent. But in the end she must go
through the fire alone.

Eva's relationship to me is indicated by the fox looking in through
the opening in the upper left side of the fence that isolates her. Eva
said that the little fox symbolizes her therapist. Eva felt that I too had
been inside the fire and would be capable of recognizing the process
within her. Because the fox is well-known for his cunning or slyness,
his sense of scent and his clear vision during the night, he appears
often in dreams and sand pictures as a symbol for the therapist,
guiding the soul.[35] The fox's red color also associates him with fire—
and the devil! In placing the little fox here, Eva showed that she had

faith in my ability to accompany her through the fires of hell. Perhaps the inner fox within her own psyche was also watching over the process.

Eva's Thirteenth Sand Picture

Illustration 28

Fire was the dominant element in the previous picture with Eva in the fire of transformation. Now we see, with some surprise and sense of redemption, a refreshingly tranquil country scene where the earth element predominates: Green plants are growing and the fertile earth brings forth life.

We recall the powerful image of the earth-mother and her house in Eva's third sand picture (Illustration 18). It was then that the archetype of the good earth was constellated. Now, almost a year later, we can see the effects of these energies on Eva's daily life. At first the theme expressed archetypically by the earth-mother was then still far from consciousness, but now it is expressed in images which are much close to consciousness: the 'good earth' is presented in the form of healthy, fertile, everyday country life.

In the middle of the sand picture is a large, comfortable farm house. Its mighty roof protects and contains its residents, just as a good mother would. A small child in a stroller is cared for by the grandparents. A man works in the woods (lower edge) and a woman feeds the cows and sheep. Behind the house there are flowers and fruits of the field. Two fish swim in the nearby creek.

The entire scene depicts a supportive family situation which Eva would have benefited from as a child but which only now has been formed in the therapeutic process. A similar theme is portrayed in the lower right corner (viewed in terms of spatial symbology, this is the quadrant of the personal mother relationship). There, we see a round, motherly feminine figure which sits hidden in the greenery. She feeds and cares for two children, one light and one dark. This little group suggests that Eva now feels that as a whole person, her bright and light, and her dark, somber sides are accepted by a mother. Perhaps due to her feeling of being accepted by her therapist, her fellow human beings, or simply 'the world', she can now accept both sides of herself.

The whole greening, fertile picture expresses that Eva has come to 'the good earth' and can now grow. Much like a seed which has fallen on fertile soil she can put down roots. Only by being born into concrete reality, by having gained a foothold on Earth, is upward, spiritually based growth made possible. In the upper left corner of the sand tray, which symbolizes the space for the spiritual, religious life, we can see the beginning of this development. On freshly tilled soil doves have come to peck for food. Doves are ancient symbols for spirituality, inspiration, and sublimated eros.[36] Indeed, this is a hopeful picture prefiguring Eva's future development!

After the long series of pictures of suffering of which we have seen only a selection, this picture had special meaning, not only for Eva but also for me as her analyst. As I mentioned earlier, as psychically active sources of energy, the effects of some sand pictures may not become visible in the daily life of the analysand until months later. Since Eva's condition had been fraught with psychic instability and dissolving tendencies, I felt this picture indicated that Eva's ego was re-forming and stabilizing. Figuratively speaking, after the long dark period of suffering a new birth appeared in a healthy green, life supporting setting.

The scene in the upper right corner belongs to this 'green' motif as well. Eva saw this as the realm of the vegetation goddess, the 'verdant one'. She is crowned with flowers and leaves and stands in front of her castle. A small, yellow figure enters her realm.

The male equivalent of Eva's female 'verdant one' is better known. For example, the vegetation god, Khidr, is the mysterious, Islamic servant of God. He is called the 'eternal youth' or the 'verdant one'.[37] In Islam, green is a sacred color symbolizing life. Human life processes 'are green' in the sense of developing their inherent potentials in slow, difficult and at first incomprehensible ways. As Jung has stated, the ineluctable urge and compulsion to self-realization is a law of nature and thus of invincible power.[38]

Plate 1. *Eva's First Sand Picture, discussed on pages 54–58.*

Plate 2. *Eva's Second Sand Picture, discussed on pages 58–60.*

Plate 3. *Eva's Third Sand Picture, discussed on pages 60–61.*

Plate 4. *Eva's Fourth Sand Picture, discussed on pages 61–63.*

Plate 5. *Eva's Fifth Sand Picture, discussed on pages 63-64.*

Plate 6. *Eva's Sixth Sand Picture, discussed on pages 64-65.*

Plate 7. *Eva's Seventh Sand Picture, discussed on pages 65-67.*

Plate 8. *Eva's Eighth Sand Picture, discussed on page 67.*

Plate 9. *Eva's Ninth Sand Picture, discussed on pages 68-69.*

Plate 10. *Eva's Tenth Sand Picture, discussed on pages 69-70.*

Plate 11. *Eva's Eleventh Sand Picture, discussed on page 71.*

Plate 12. *Eva's Twelfth Sand Picture, discussed on pages 71-73.*

Plate 13. *Eva's Thirteenth Sand Picture, discussed on pages 73–75.*

Plate 14. *Eva's Fourteenth Sand Picture, discussed on page 76.*

Plate 15. *Eva's Fifteenth Sand Picture, discussed on page 76.*

Plate 16. *Eva's Sixteenth Sand Picture, discussed on pages 77–78.*

Plate 17. *Maria's First Sand Picture, discussed on pages 86–88.*

Plate 18. *Maria's Second Sand Picture, discussed on pages 88–90.*

Plate 19. *Maria's Third Sand Picture, discussed on pages 90–91.*

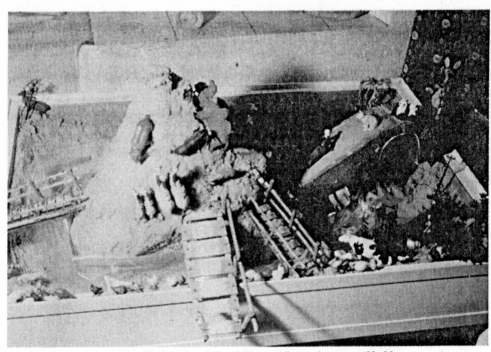

Plate 20. *Maria's Fourth Sand Picture, discussed on pages 92–93.*

Plate 21. *Maria's Fifth Sand Picture, discussed on pages 93–96.*

Plate 22. *Maria's Sixth Sand Picture, discussed on pages 93–96.*

Plate 23. *Maria's Seventh Sand Picture, discussed on pages 96–97.*

Plate 24. *The Ladybug, discussed on page 87.*

Plate 25. *Elizabeth, The Chief Figures.*

Plate 26. *Elizabeth's First Sand Picture, discussed on pages 101–06.*

Plate 27. *Elizabeth's Second Sand Picture, discussed on pages 106–111.*

Plate 28. *Elizabeth's Third Sand Picture, discussed on pages 111–12.*

Plate 29. *Elizabeth's Fourth Sand Picture, discussed on page 113.*

Plate 30. *Elizabeth's Fifth Sand Picture, discussed on pages 113–15.*

Plate 31. *Elizabeth's Sixth Sand Picture, discussed on pages 115–16.*

Plate 32. *Elizabeth's Seventh Sand Picture, discussed on pages 116–19.*

I had made this green, 'feminine' goddess myself, years ago, because I felt that for sandplay I needed a figure which would represent the essence of the verdant, vegetative life in outer nature, as well as in the inner nature of the person. We take this level of life for granted, so much so that we mismanage and neglect it or even despise it as 'lower' or 'unspiritual'. But for me it is most important because this level is the nourishing, the supporting foundation of our life. Mankind's spirit must ultimately be rooted there as well. There is a very real danger that without a grounding in concrete, realistic structures, spirit lifts off and detaches itself from the earth. Needless to say, such a split between body and spirit is most unhealthy. (It might be clear now that sandplay may be the therapeutic method for persons who suffer from precisely such a split!)

The green, verdant figure is thus intimately tied to me and my convictions. The yellow figure embodies Eva. Both figures in this sand picture represent the existing transference situation between Eva and myself. Without needing to express this verbally, the analysand feels that the analyst is filled with the positive energy of the green, verdant divinity. A deep and close alliance prevails during a long and intensive analysis. During this time the analyst communicates with the analysand nonverbally, by his attitude, both the knowledge of and trust in the meaningfulness of life's processes. The analyst's example creates a response in the analysand, a sympathetic resonance, which in the present case was found to be a healing factor.

Illustration 29

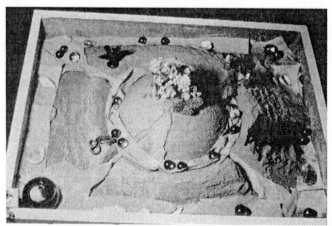

Eva's Fourteenth Sand Picture

Here we meet once again the motif of resonance. On the lower left
edge of the sand tray sits a blue mermaid who plays the harp. She is
linked with the central female figure who is surrounded by flowers
and represents Eva's ego. Music and flowers symbolize the deep
feeling of resolution and redemption, but also the genuine feelings of
mourning which filled Eva after the long tense time of suffering. Her
seemingly unending rivers of tears fill this entire landscape of her
soul. The moat surrounding the central hill is filled and the outer dike
which up to now had protected but also isolated Eva has been
opened. It appears that Eva wishes to dissolve the old structures of
her personality by washing them off. This is a process of inner
purification; it is an ablution and an immersion in one's own waters
of renewal.

Eva's Fifteenth Sand Picture

Illustration 30

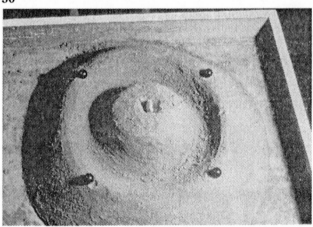

This picture is a simple but extremely concentrated representation of
a profound event. The outer structure is a quaternity, the basic
structure of psychic orientation.[39] Out of the depth of its center rises
quintessentially the white fish of the soul. We have met with this fish
before in Illustration 22 where it was connected to Eva's own grave.
After many months working on a process of transformation the fish
appears once again as a symbol of Eva's reborn psyche.

Eva's Sixteenth Sand Picture

Illustration 31

It's a sunny day! This last picture of the series possesses a very special beauty and expressiveness. One is reminded of Eva's forming the primordial hill in the first sand picture (Illustration 16), which represented a spontaneously formed mandala. Furthermore, the central sun motif is reminiscent of the impressive archetypal sun image (Illustration 17). Here we see a perfectly centered mandala, but this time it is one which has been modelled most consciously. Out of the elevated sun image emanate various concentric circles similar to waves in water.

Eva commented that "the sun symbolizes the light and the power of divine consciousness. Rays emanate from there like hands which touch the world until they reach the people. The spheres are the still unformed, free-flowing energy between the sun and the world." (Eva did not know the Celtic description of the river or water world as subtle, moving energy. Nevertheless, I have come across such glass spheres in the sand pictures of other analysands and there they served also as an expression of yet unformed, potential energy.) Eva continued, "The green circle represents the earth. There the rays touch the people. The seashells behind the human figures are the protective shields against the outermost circle which is the devouring unconscious represented by reptiles, crocodiles and archaic monsters. From the lower left edge humans grow slowly, counterclockwise, out of the earth. With them also grows the protective shield. The hands of the sun which are the rays of divine consciousness touch the people. With growing human consciousness also grows the protective shield against the fears and horror of the 'night', for example, the fears which arise in a person's own unconscious."

Eva's significant commentary speaks for itself. But when we look at the sand picture more closely we can see yet another important detail: the seashells behind the human figures act as reflectors. The rays of the sun, that is, of divine consciousness, are reflected back after they have been transformed through mankind. Each individual transforms the divine energy in a personal way and reflects it back to its origin. We can also express this reciprocal action and reaction between god and man by suggesting that the energies of the archetypal images influence and change the person whereupon the transformed person influences and changes the forms of the archetypal image. There is a reciprocity between the archetypal images and the individual as well as between the archetypal images and the collective. This is especially true of the great fields of archetypal energy in a culture, for example the dominant God-image, which is so influential at the level of both the individual and the collective. From this point of view, creative imagination and the related expansion of consciousness of the individual is of the utmost significance. It contributes—for good or ill—to the creating of the world or 'world making' as well as to the further development of the collective consciousness. The personal ethical responsiblity of each individual is decisive for its positive or negative effect on this world making.

Once again, on an inner psychic level we find the principle of resonance. Here it is the resonance between the higher wholeness, Eva's Self and Eva's emergent and still growing ego consciousness. The eight figures in the sand picture represent the eight different stages of the growth of Eva's conscious personality.

We might view the figure-eight in this picture as a static principle of order, as a new beginning after a completed term. 'Eight' stands for the eighth day of creation, that is, the new creation beginning with the birth of Christ.[40] What is symbolized here is the new beginning, Eva's rebirth into a more robust and conscious way of being.

This synoptic and radiant sand picture was not the last sand picture but it marked the union of Eva's unconscious process in sandplay with her conscious life. It indicated the beginning of the second part of Eva's therapeutic process, the verbal part. Now was the time for the conscious confrontation of Eva with herself, her environment and her image of God. In the space of a few months, of her own free will, she put aside both alcohol and medication and turned her attention increasingly toward her family and her professional training.

In conclusion, we can compare the steps in Eva's developmental process to the individual steps of a psychologically interpreted alchemical process. Here I follow Jung's text from *Psychology and Alchemy*, very closely:

> The *nigredo* or blackness is the initial state, either present from the beginning . . . , or else produced by the separation . . . of the elements. If the separated condition is assumed at the start, as sometimes happens, then a union of opposites is performed under the likeness of a union of male and female (called the . . . *conjunctio* . . .), followed by the death of the product of the union (*mortificatio* . . .) and a corresponding nigredo. From this the washing (*ablutio* . . .) either leads directly to the whitening (*albedo*), or else the soul . . . released at the "death" is reunited with the dead body and brings about its resurrection . . . At this point the main goal of the process is reached, namely the albedo . . . , highly prized by many alchemists as if it were the ultimate goal. It is the silver or moon condition, which still has to be raised to the sun condition. The albedo is, so to speak, the daybreak, but not till the *rubedo* is it the sunrise.[41]

The *nigredo* condition was present in Eva at the beginning of therapy. During the long and dark months of her depression she experienced herself as dismembered and dissociated. After beginning therapy at the sand tray, the first union of opposites was constellated at the archetypal level (see Illustrations 20 and 21). These culminated in the representation of the crucified Christ. With such a union of energies as a base there followed, again for months, the transition through the *nigredo* and the *mortificatio*. During this time Eva encountered her darkness and her suffering and finally the subsequent death and dissolution of her previous personality. In the deepest darkness there came the turning point. On the ascent, healing and rebirth began (see Illustration 25). As a consequence, Eva's newly born ego had to undergo baptism by fire in order to become more robust and take root in the fertile, maternal earth (see Illustrations 27 and 28). Illustration 29 shows us the cleansing and dissolving power through the torrent of tears. Here the remains of the old ego are washed away by a genuine experience of mourning. The *ablutio* in alchemy is sometimes also called *baptisma*, which refers to the cleansing power of baptismal water. The rising of the light at daybreak, the *albedo*, or the whitening as it was also called, is symbolized by the white fish of the soul in Illustration 30 after we had first encountered the same symbol in the seventh sand picture (Illustration 22). At that time the fish represented the as yet secret knowledge in Eva's unconscious soul that the positive energies would in the end prevail over the negative ones. What we experience in the last sand picture (Illustration 31) is the *rubedo*, the actual sunrise. Here it is a symbol for a 'new day' in Eva's life. It means that Eva possesses a new conscious outlook on life. The picture also represents, however, a second *conjunctio*, this time the union of opposites of conscious and unconscious, ego and Self.

As I have indicated, at the time these new emergent energies became available to Eva because of her experiential process, her therapy was by no means completed. We were able to close the great wound of her early narcissistic disturbance. The healing of such an early injury in the deepest levels of Eva's personality was a necessary condition for the later confrontation with herself and her environment. This lengthy process, requiring great patience and perseverance by Eva and myself, was only the beginning work 'at the roots'. We know that the loveliest traits in a plant cannot develop without healthy roots. Had we not been able to heal Eva's narcissistic wound, all of her talents and mental abilities, so evident in her sand pictures, would have had but little chance of further development. But this plant image for the psychic healing process is only partially valid for what happens in reality. This image remains entirely in nature, whereas a therapeutic process is cultural, a *conscious* working together of analyst and analysand. In Eva's case, the first phase of her healing process was primarily nonverbal and unconscious for the analysand. Her conscious wish and will to get well was strengthened in that she regularly confronted her unconscious in creative designs and formations in the sand tray. The analyst, on the contrary, must consciously know what is going on in the analysand. The analytic art lies in expressing only as much as is absolutely necessary. Because the analytic work is a natural process of growth, a process of cultivation, I return to the image of building the house of the soul. Earlier, I compared the analyst to the construction foreman. But he cannot become the architect of the house of the soul, for that function belongs to the inner, directing authority of the analysand. The construction foreman or analyst must be able to comprehend the plans of this inner authority and facilitate the construction. He may need to intervene if mistakes are being made. He does make a significant contribution to the construction of the house of the soul of his analysand by virtue of his knowledge and ability.

Eva's experiential process at the sand tray centered on building the foundation of the house of her psyche. This was primarily an underground process, occurring in the unconscious at the level of earliest childhood where conscious access is quite limited. Above ground, in Eva's daily life, one could intuit that something was going on underneath, but this became visible only very gradually. Sand pictures may anticipate by months, perhaps even years, the person's external development. Such 'subterranean work' in the sand is, however, absolutely necessary. It provides the signposts and the energy for the later phases of conscious work on oneself. This was also true in Eva's case. Eva's conscious personality, or what became visible above the ground of Eva's house of the soul was the product of her subsequent verbal analysis. This development was possible only because the foundation had been laid during the earlier, mostly unconsciously experienced sandplay process.

Maria: The Healing Process in a Child

After presenting the difficult healing process in an adult woman, I would now like to present the first pictures of a child in therapy. I will not give an exhaustive analysis of the entire course of her therapy, which I have already described elsewhere,[42] but rather I would like to show how the movement of psychic energy is especially prominent in one child's pictures. I do not know where else the movements upward and downward and the regression and progression of energy can be seen better than in the three dimensions of sandplay.

The sandplay method is extraordinarily suited for children because they still possess an unbroken delight in creative play and modelling and also because they still have a natural understanding for the symbolic language of the figures they use, which allows them to balance outer and inner reality in play.

Although sandplay therapies with children are as intensive as those of adults, they are less complicated and take less time since the causes of childhood disturbances do not yet lie in a long forgotten past, nor are they overlaid, as they would be in an adult, with secondary problems.

Maria was seven years old and in her first year of school when she came to me for therapy. She was the first-born child in the family, willful and active, ahead of her peers intellectually, and physically very healthy. But for some time now she had been acting very aggressively at home. She was often argumentative and had difficulties in expressing herself. She thought she was ugly and did not like herself. She had difficulty in adjusting socially. She was also afraid of water and everything that was new, for example the walk to school and recess. When she started school, it became apparent that she did not love or trust herself. There must have been a disturbance in her primal relationship to her mother, which inhibited her development as she left infancy and started school.

The main difficulty in Maria's family was that everything masculine was overvalued, including rational thought and every kind of goal-oriented intellectual achievement. Consequently the feminine values, such as trust in one's instinct and in one's body and

83

psychic life, were poorly developed. This had been a source of great distress for Maria's mother during the transitional period when she shifted from her intellectual, academic world to being a mother. Being the first child, Maria was deeply affected by her mother's insecurity. It was all the more impressive, then, to see how the transformation and strengthening of Maria's personality through therapy in turn affected the entire family, resulting in their positive change and development.

After a discussion with Maria's parents during which we paid careful attention to her previous development, her difficulties, and the family background, it was decided that Maria should come for therapy every week for an hour. We left it up to Maria whether she would like to play in the sand tray or not. But when she came for her first hour she went immediately, as if driven, to the sand tray and the shelves with the miniature figures. She took up a large, wooden kangaroo and a hideous crocodile. The crocodile pursued the kangaroo all around the tray. Maria said the evil crocodile wanted to devour the kind kangaroo. After that she created her first sand picture.

What does this initial motif tell us? Certainly, we are faced with two striking opposites: an evil part intent on devouring a kind part. The kangaroo, representing the kind part, is often used as a symbol for the containment of the small child in a protective, warm, nourishing motherly environment, so necessary during early childhood. It expresses for children not only the physical, but also the psychic support offered by a mother and the warm feeling experienced in a positive mother-child relationship.

A positive primal relationship with the mother (or in some circumstances the father) not only provides the foundation for the child's relationships to his body but also for his interpersonal relationships, that's to say, all his emotional relatedness to other people. Healthy ego development as well as healthy relationships to the 'thou', the world, the ego's own unconscious, and the self depend on a positive primal relationship to the mother figure.[43]

We can see how important it is that the child has a successful primal relationship with the mother, which in this case appears in the symbol of the kangaroo. In this relationship the child experiences a feeling of primal trust in life. But life means confrontation, a dramatic experience of one's body, soul, family, school, and the 'big outside world' with all its joys and suffering, hopes and fears. Sometimes the urge toward forward progression and self-realization is strongest. At other times, the child regresses, becoming helpless when faced with the frightful and dark sides of life. Of course, the child experiences both sides repeatedly. But a secure mother-child attachment protects and insures against being overwhelmed by the darkness. It gives the child, and later the adult, strength to experience the moments of darkness as times of inner transformations and transitions to new potentialities.

One must not forget that there is a specific time in which this mother-child unity should develop. After a certain age, to remain in this unity would mean a flight from life. What began as maternal security and protection could turn into a prison, hindering the child's development. The reason why the child cannot move forward and leave 'the pouch of the kangaroo', is usually because he has not experienced an adequate life-giving primal relationship to his mother. Sometimes the mother cannot release her child into the next period of life, yet the child is being pushed by its own development to leave this maternal environment. But the child cannot because he has not yet sufficiently experienced this maternal world and integrated its potential source of energy.

At the beginning of therapy, Maria seemed to identify with the baby kangaroo in the pouch, but felt herself persecuted by a large, threatening power, the evil crocodile.

Even children know that the crocodile lives in the water or lurks in a swamp. There it lies waiting for its prey and pulls it under the water to drown. We can therefore equate the crocodile with the devouring, fatal aspect of water, which, as we know, Maria feared greatly.

Life begins in water, but it can also end there. Man is born out of the amniotic fluid in the maternal uterus, but once having begun to breathe he cannot return totally to the water. Only in a traditional baptism can one be re-immersed in his original element and emerge symbolically reborn.

Water as a metaphor is without a doubt the main symbol for those energies which are unconscious and unformed, and one could even say, unborn. A temporary immersion in water can be refreshing. A person may experience new energies and feel revitalized. But to sink back into the water and be engulfed by it may symbolize a regression to an unconscious, formless condition. Such movement must be seen as counterproductive to development.

In her sand picture, Maria showed that she was frightened and in need. I knew from her life history that her early relationship with her mother was inadequate. Therefore, she lacked the trust and strength to move forward. On the other hand, her sand picture indicated that she felt threatened and pursued by a crocodile, that is, she was in danger of regressing into an unconscious state, or possibly a psychic or physical illness.

Psychotherapy offers a child the protected space in which he can return symbolically to the waters of the maternal uterus. Here he can relive the vital primal mother-child relationship, but this time with the therapist. This, however, will succeed only if the therapist can fully accept, protect and guide the child during this regression and accompany him in the subsequent reconstruction of his personality.

Let us now take a look at the first sand picture Maria created, but let us not forget that play for a child is not 'just play', but real life.

Maria's First Sand Picture

Illustration 32

At first glance the picture seems somewhat disorderly but both the activities and shapes in the sand tray express a strong imagination and an intense emotional life.

This sand picture shows no human figures, only animals. It therefore represents the animal stage of the child's development. During much of this time the child is unconsciously or preconsciously involved in the world of the body, the instincts, the drives, and emotions. The animals represent various active, moving and mobile aspects of this world. The plants, on the other hand, are strongly rooted in the earth. Thus, they embody the vegetative stage of the child's development. This occurs during approximately the first year of life.

In the center of the picture rises a round hill, almost like a first elevation rising from Maria's unconscious life. This hill reminds us of nature almost arching, wishing to break open in order to release a small sprout eager to emerge. We can compare this sprout to the growing ego of the child which grows out of Mother Earth during the course of development, leaving its unconscious darkness for the light of the world. There it begins to see.

When an opening in the earth forms, the emerging sprout points upward and connects to the light, to heaven. The transition from one form of existence into another is made possible. One can express a connection between heaven and earth with a mountain, which would bring the person closer to heaven, or by a ladder, a tree, or the world pillar.[44] This world pillar is always 'in the center', the axis or navel of the world; it is also the center of the personal world, no matter how large or small this world may be in the individual person. Every sand picture represents this individual world of the world-creating person. Thus, in Maria's picture the hill represents her personal world axis, her connection between heaven and earth. The crocodile is lying on this mountain. It is a threat to everything which wants to come to the light. This means that the crocodile, representing the devouring aspect of her unconscious, prevents Maria's upward growth, her development toward a more differentiated consciousness.

Toward the left of crocodile hill is a small canal which leads toward the lower right corner and empties into a small lake. A large green boat moves in the canal, powered from behind by a dangerous snake. In the boat stands a ladybug with a small umbrella. That figure is the only one in the entire sand picture which is even remotely reminiscent of anything human. It is standing above the other animals. Maria uses the ladybug in almost each of the following pictures. She thought she was the little bug (Illustration 39). Consequently, this figure has a central meaning.

Let us look at the boat in which the ladybug rides. The function of ships, cars, and sleds (see the next sand picture, Illustration 33) is to transport people or goods from one place to another. In various religions the god-image was carried in such vehicles. These vehicles always express movement, transit, a rite of passage.[45] The movement from one grade level to the next in school is a rite of passage par excellence. In Maria's case we were concerned with her passage from the toddler's world to the more conscious world of the primary school age child. This transitional time is one of the more difficult and important periods in a child's development. This is when the child must move from the 'natural', unconscious, animal, or physical existence to a higher, religious, spiritual and cultural life which makes us human.

I think it is legitimate to view the wide, green boat as an expression of Maria's 'natural' way of being. The ladybug stands in the boat as a symbol of Maria's preconscious ego. The boat is driven by the snake, on its way to the lake. There the waters of the lake envelop the

fish and ducklings as a mother would her children. The lake
represents the primordial situation, the containment in the maternal
uterus. For Maria this means a regression to an earlier stage, the
mother-child relationship which, during the therapeutic situation,
she must relive symbolically.

Every sand picture is a multi-layered formation and expresses
various psychic situations and energy movements simultaneously.
The two main movements in this first sand picture are the upward
movements of growth, which are blocked by the crocodile, and the
regressive movement symbolizing a return to the mother-child unity.
It appears obvious that Maria knew unconsciously what she needed
to do. It was necessary first to return to the mother-child unity stage
where she could be sufficiently nurtured and regain a basic sense of
trust in life. This would then provide the ground for her spiritual and
mental growth.

Maria's Second Sand Picture

Illustration 33

After a week Maria created her second picture. It feels open, light,
and clear, as if her problems were being laid open to the world. The
movement at the lower edge of the tray is striking: arriving animals
and small cars mark a movement from the left toward the center.
Energy flows from the unconscious into a central hollow, and there
we also find the ladybug. In the hollow is a collection of light and dark
animals; some are even black and white. This shows the beginning of
an inner differentiation into opposites: light-dark, good-evil are
necessary for the development of a discerning consciousness.

The action on the small hill in the upper center of the tray contrasts with the events described above. There, small rabbits sit under palm trees. In front sits a yellow mouse on a sled which is being pulled by a donkey toward the left, away from the central action.

The donkey seems to be an important animal for Maria. We encountered him already in the first sand picture at the left edge and we will see him again in the next pictures. The donkey is the less appreciated brother of the horse. If one cannot own a horse, one can at least own a donkey, to work and carry heavy loads. The donkey is tough and enduring, but also tenacious and obstinate. That is his way of defending himself against abuse. Perhaps children think a donkey is stupid. A common epithet is, after all, 'You stupid ass!' Many children might actually feel sorry for a donkey because he suffers from mistreatment by the adults. Surely, children identify with the donkey because they too suffer when adults scorn their youthful ignorance or presumed stupidity, just like a donkey's. It may be comforting when children read about a poor donkey who was redeemed from his pitiable existence and finds a loving pasture somewhere.

Equally comforting to a child may be the relationship between the donkey and the divine, or the Christ-figure. The donkey lies next to the manger during Christ's birth. Also, the donkey carries Christ as a child and as an adult. Children see this in picture books and illustrated Bibles. Children are still close to God. Unless this feeling has been spoiled for them, they have a simple and healthy feeling for the divine. Thus, I believe that children identify with the donkey who must suffer in this world but who is close to God. One could also say that in general, the donkey represents the suffering and endurance of one's shadow sides, which, however, may lead to salvation and wholeness.

The donkey in the story of Pinocchio[46] was especially important to Maria. There the ass was first a jumping jack, just an animated piece of wood. After countless adventures he became a real boy who learned how to read and write, he became knowledgeable. In the story twelve donkeys pull the wagon which brings Pinocchio to the land of the children. There "the children did not need to learn anything, they only played." Pinocchio too only wanted to play and laugh and in due course became a little donkey himself. But then he became very sad because of it. His sadness made him want to learn. Thereupon he was redeemed from his asinine condition.

Because Maria identified with the story of Pinocchio, we can say that the donkey in the sand picture represents that aspect of her personality which did not wish to develop but to remain an ignorant little girl. Because her development stopped at the animal stage, her entire personality suffered. But this suffering now became the motivating force for Maria's further development.

Returning to the sand picture, we can see the donkey pulling the sled with the little mouse, which represents, as I have suggested, Maria's infant soul.[47] He pulls it away from the center toward the left, toward the unconscious. In this sand picture we see psychic energy moving regressively from the center toward the left, but at the same time there is a noticeable influx of energies from the left toward the center, which builds consciousness.

Maria's Third Sand Picture

Illustration 34

Another week passed and Maria made her third sand picture. What is striking here is the height and depth of the sand formations. The picture gives the impression of uprootedness; it seems filled with turmoil and emotions. Again, one is struck by the fact that fish and crocodiles swim in the water out of which rises a tall, steep mountain. On top of the mountain perches the ladybug, in a most precarious position. It must have gotten lost and can't find its way down. There are two bridges leading to the foot of the mountain but there is no trail to the top. Maria's little ego, having lost its way, seems isolated and in distress. This position is aptly illustrated by Erich Neumann's concept of the 'distress-ego':

> A child's negative distress-ego is the expression of a pathologically reinforced ego into which it has been forced and in which it must

subsist on its own resources though not equipped by nature and its stage of development to do so. Behind such forced and violent self-assertion there is always anxiety, forsakenness, and a lack of trust embracing the entire sphere of what is normally contained in the primal relationship, namely, the child's relation to the thou, the world, its own unconscious, and the self.[48]

As a counter-movement to the distressing situation in which Maria's ego finds itself, there is the yellow fish in a blue boat, in the bottom of a circular pond. If we recall the ladybug in the green boat of the first sand picture, which floated back to the maternal pond, then we can see a new development here, a development most likely caused by the spiritual-maternal love and devotion of the therapist toward Maria. The little fish appears like a harbinger of Maria's new personality, which now travels in a spiritual boat (blue is the color of heaven, the spirit).[49]

Maria's Fourth Sand Picture

Illustration 35

In this picture, the four bridges stand out. They stand over the edge of the sand tray and lead to the central mountain. They represent the flow of energy from the outside, for example, from the countertransference of the therapist to the patient. If the therapist brings positive feelings to the child and expects positive things in return, the child's talents and personality may grow and blossom. This interaction is like a bridge the child can cross over to find himself. This was certainly the case with Maria. I liked Maria very much, which she certainly sensed although she didn't pay any attention to me, concentrating totally on the sandplay.

Various animals come from the right side. Maria related to them with warmth and love; that is, they represented positive energies. Also on the mountain we find rising, positive energies represented by zebras, camels, and mountain goats. But despite the flow of these helpful energies Maria still suffered from her early lack of primal relationship. Her fear and anxiety continued to push her sprouting ego back into an unconscious condition.

Such transitional periods require our utmost attention. For the analysand it is a most difficult time when the new personality shows itself 'in embryo' as it were, but is not yet strong enough to go on to certain further developments. In his 'The Psychology of the Trans-ference', Jung commented on this critical stage of analysis when the conscious mind is liable to be submerged at any moment in the unconscious. During such disorientation the precious substance, the soul of the analysand, is in danger of escaping. "This precious substance is a paradoxical composite of fire and water, i.e., Mercurius, the *servus* or *cervus fugitivus* (the fugitive stag) who is ever about to flee—or who, in other words, resists integration (into consciousness)."[50]

The precious substance of the soul is, like a fugitive stag, constantly in search of an escape, that is, it resists integration into consciousness. This assertion contains a helpful hint concerning the very strange and altogether unchildlike motif of the two stags in Maria's sand picture. A stag appears at the lower right, and one at the upper left. Both are characterized as light-figures because of a lamp standing near them. The upper left stag appears to wish to leave the sand picture and we are therefore entitled to call him the 'fugitive stag'. We can also gather from the location of the stags within the space of the sand tray that there is a movement afoot in the direction of spiritual development in Maria's psyche (see my guide for the symbolic interpretation of spatial phenomena in Chapter 5 above). It should be noted, however, that this movement from the lower right to the upper left has no goal, but takes place outside the sand tray in empty space. There was an obvious danger that the stag which symbolizes the light of a higher level of consciousness might again leave Maria's world. In other words, there was the danger that Maria's emergent ego-consciousness might not be strong enough and that the 'crocodile' would continue to block her development.

This sand picture then is a clear indication that the countertrans-ference had given rise to an influx of positive energies. These energies had been transferred from me as Maria's therapist to Maria. But they would need careful nurturing in order to be maintained and to be able to continue to protect and strengthen Maria's budding ego.

Maria's Fifth and Sixth Sand Pictures

Illustration 36

Once again, after a week, Maria modelled the fifth and sixth sand pictures. They are so closely related that I wish to interpret them jointly.

In the fifth picture coming from the right, to the left edge of the sixth picture there is a great movement of energy which expresses new archetypal themes. This energy flows out and on toward the next thematic circle until we come to a wheel dug into the sand representing an even deeper and more unconscious level. The wheel is not only the object farthest to the left but lies at the deepest level of both pictures. We can imagine that the energies are not spread uniformly over the surface area. Rather, these energies are like the waters of a fountain flowing from higher levels into various lower basins. Each basin is like a round bowl or like a child's developmental level where the energies are gathered until the bowl is filled, when they flow over into the next one below. Thus, the energies course through the developmental stages of the child in retrograde motion back to the beginning. If, on the other hand, we start from the lowest point of the sand picture, that is, at the wheel, then the movement describes an ascent from stage to stage. Such movements occur in many creation myths, for example, the myths narrated by the Hopi

Illustration 37

Indians. There, the development of human culture is described as an ascent through various world planes.

The central circle in the fifth picture takes the form of a flat hollow which is filled to the brim with domestic animals. All of them contribute to mankind's nutrition and warmth. The picture radiates a fulfilling, nurturing, warm, and good motherliness. It is the fulfilling aspect of the positive mother archetype, in which the ladybug is included as well. In the very center of the circle Maria placed a large owl with her daughter and Maria indicated that I was the mother owl and she her daughter—this very circle is now a manifestation of the life-giving primal relationship, the mother-child unity, so important for Maria.

From this circle the energies flow farther to the left to the adjacent circle. Here a little man tames wild animals. In a child we can be certain that taming wild forces touches upon the problem of raising children, or education in the largest sense. It is most interesting that after this 'taming of the circus', Maria created a ditch at the lower right, the most shaded corner of the picture. Into this ditch she put a wild sow. Without hesitation Maria hold me that at home she sometimes acted like a wild sow. [Translator's note: The Swiss-German idiom, 'to let loose the wild sow', means that a person will be furious and possibly destructive.] Maria said that during such times she would rage and yell and would like to smash everything to pieces.

Education here is compared to the taming of wild animals and is seen in contrast to the wild sow. This shows quite clearly that during the formation of the child from a natural being into an adjusted, 'civilized' member of society, the wild sow might appear; that is, wild, destructive emotionality accompanies this transition. Being nice, orderly, and well-behaved, accepting the rhythm and lifestyle of the adults requires repressing the 'bad' character traits. In Maria's case they were the wild and untamed emotions which would return and erupt suddenly and disturb the peace in the family.

Let us focus on the circle to the right in the sixth picture. Here the opposites of tamed animals and wild animals are united. In the middle stand two madonna figures, one made of silver, the other of gold. This whole circle represents the 'Great Mother' as the mistress of the animals, or of animal life,[51]—and the energies flow further toward a new circle.

Here, under the trees, are small animals, rabbits, and chickens, belonging to the fertile earth. In this circle of vegetative life[52] stands the ladybug, representing Maria's feminine ego and a little man who probably represents her masculine side. They are together and united. From this vegetative realm the energies flow onward, that is, two donkeys lead us to the place where, in abstract form, the opposites of male and female are represented. To the left there is an erect pole, a phallic, male symbol. To the right we find an earthen jug and a water hole. Because of the uterine form we have no trouble seeing in the earthen jug a symbol of the primordial feminine. The water hole is the fundamental condition for the origin of life. If we take the point of view of mankind located here upon the Earth, the water hole symbolizes the emergence of humankind from the maternal primordial water onto the Earth, his place of concrete, material existence. The pole, located on this Earth, symbolizes the ascent, the upward climb to the patriarchal world of the spirit and heaven. The retrograde motion, the descent, however, is symbolized as well. We climb back down to Earth for re-immersion into the water. There the movement begins again. Re-immersion is therefore not a death but a rebirth.[53] This eternal cycle of becoming and passing away is symbolized by the wheel that stands in the sand and reaches down to the bottom of the sand tray which, as I have said earlier, represents water. This wheel looks very much like a water wheel which brings up water for the irrigation of the fields. We can compare this picture with the human psyche that continuously draws new contents from the unconscious and brings them to light.

But why should it be two *donkeys* which lead to the wheel? If we recall my earlier comments about the symbolism of the donkey then we must understand that the wheel turns and the raising of consciousness continues as long as a person suffers from his own unconsciousness and ignorance, precisely his asininity, and strives for the realization of the Self. Here the situation is the same as it was in the second sand picture. It is the suffering caused by Maria's own unconsciousness, here symbolized by the donkey, which is the leading force of her development process.

Maria was unaware of all of these connections, but she had reached her 'primordial waters'. She was able to go forward and reconstruct her personality from there.

Maria's Seventh Sand Picture

Illustration 38

We see an impressive line of cows and horses moving in a broad, dynamic movement swinging from the lower right toward the left and then returning toward the upper right. Looking at this place-ment in the sand tray, we see the flow of the movement as coming from the realm of the maternal (lower right) toward the left, the inner world. There, the movement changes directions and flows, past the ladybug, again toward the right, the realm of the family and larger environment. So the energy flows backwards, only to culminate in a large, progressive forward movement.

The cows symbolize the nourishing, warmth-giving maternal aspect. As I see it, there seems to be a relationship between these cows and the circle of the 'Good Mother' of the fifth picture. The horses express vitality and dynamism and would connect to the circle of the 'animal life' of the sixth picture. Both these circles were filled with bundled potential energy. At this point they change into directed energy and make the great forward movement possible. Now Maria was able to enter her new stage of life.

If we look at Maria's growth while she was making the first seven

Illustration 39

The Ladybug (In German, Marienkäfer—*Maria's beetle)*

pictures, we see that she was guided by an *inner*, goal-directed, ordering knowledge. Through this inner guidance, with the therapist's assistance, and in the 'free and protected space' of therapy, her once blocked energy was freed. Through the next 33 hours of therapy Maria was able to develop a healthy ego and a stronger personality.

In order to provide an atmosphere of devotion and trust in the free and protected space of the therapy room, the therapist must be completely open to the child and have no preconceptions about the course of therapy. Nor should the therapist expect the child to achieve certain results within a specific time. Only then can the child open up without anxiety and develop the necessary trust and confidence. The therapist must protect the closeness of the relationship, the weaving of transference and countertransference, so it is not carried outside. The therapist must trust in the self-healing tendencies in the soul of the child, but must also observe this ongoing process closely in order to intervene, if necessary. If these conditions can be created then both the therapeutic space and the sand tray turn into the 'hermetic vessel', the former figuratively, the latter concretely. Both of these become the psychic-spiritual vessel of renewal and rebirth.

During the second part of therapy we were able to slowly open this 'hermetic vessel'. Maria and I confronted each other and this allowed Maria to try out and strengthen her transformed personality step by step. In the third phase of Maria's therapy, her strong feelings for me, her spiritual mother, were slowly dissolved. During those last hours she instinctively found her way to the garden and nature and I guided her feelings for me toward this 'Greater Mother'. In this way the vessel containing our common work was completely opened and Maria and I bade farewell to each other.

Elizabeth: A Process of Feminine Transformation

Elizabeth was 40 years old when she came to me for analysis. She was happily married and the mother of three children between the ages of 10 and 16. Having recently returned to study for a professional degree, she was now faced with her first examinations. At this juncture in life her problems could be summed up as follows: she wanted to complete a course of studies in preparation for a new profession. She sincerely felt that she could succeed in her academic training and achieve her professional goals. At the same time she feared that she might not pass her examinations and felt she was too 'dumb' for academic work. Moreover, she felt guilty towards both her husband and children because her studies did not allow her to fulfill her role of the ever-present housewife in the same way as before. Increasingly, her growing education and independence made her husband insecure. His accustomed role as 'knowing male' and *pater familias* was being challenged, and this created inner difficulties for him. Her own dilemma was no less serious. After all, she was pushed forward by her urge for development and held back by her anxieties and guilt. This produced feelings of total blocking and she wanted to try to gain clarity in the face of all these conflicting forces within her, through sandplay and analysis.

At the beginning of analysis I could not correctly judge how far Elizabeth's intellectual acumen might take her. But I soon noticed that she was very perceptive and discerning, and had developed good instincts and positive feelings for herself and her environment. Such a starting point is propitious for therapy, although rare.

Elizabeth came from an artisan's family in a small town in Switzerland. Her relationship to her mother had been good and loving. This had given her a natural and healthy trust in life and her own motherhood. Her relationship to her father was somewhat more problematic in that he could not support her intellectual interests, let alone encourage her. Even in school her intellectual abilities were misjudged and she was promptly put into a remedial program. I don't want to elaborate on the reasons for this. This evaluation seemed to Elizabeth like a cruel sentence, which soon proved erroneous. She really was an intelligent girl; she later completed her teacher's training and taught for some years before and after her marriage. After her children entered school and some had reached high school, she wanted training in a new profession. This would give her as an individual a greater opportunity to structure her time and her work.

Many women today find themselves in similar situations. Such women are not at all intellectual 'bluestockings', as they were once called. Rather, it is simply a fact that the ties to family slowly loosen and new career developments become possible. Elizabeth was a very loving and agreeable wife and mother. Nonetheless, she felt a legitimate need to develop her intellectual abilities, to become better educated and to emerge from her narrow family circle and participate in a larger cultural milieu. We must remember however, that caring for a lively family and pursuing a career at the same time is an enormous responsibility. Not everyone can afford a maid or a housekeeper! From my own experience I know that while we may denigrate the life of a housewife and mother it is still more protected and comfortable than facing the confrontations and pressures of 'achievement' in the world, or satisfying the requirements of a university program. Why then do so many women take on these dual responsibilities? Rarely have I met women who have done it out of pure ambition or boredom. Most of them seemed to be motivated by a deep inner need. It is not good when the body is neglected or when the soul atrophies; it is similarly destructive when a person doesn't actively engage his mind. If a woman does not keep her mind active (which is, after all, a fundamental human need), and represses or neglects it, she becomes dissatisfied with herself and may turn aggressively against her immediate environment or even become depressed. There is a danger that she will denigrate and devalue the intellectual achievement of others or on the other hand unconsciously displace her own need onto others and demand, for example of her husband or her children, superior performance in those very same areas she herself has neglected. In the following sand pictures we shall encounter several aspects of this complex problem.

Elizabeth herself stated that in her case, her developmental process was one of finding a transition from one feminine archetype to another. With the aid of the sand pictures and much conscious reflection on her lifestyle, she wished to find new and comprehensive feminine guidelines for her life. We discussed them verbally because Elizabeth felt a need to gain clarity about the meaning of the specific figures she used and their relationship to each other. And yet it was not an intellectual exercise alone, but was always related to her daily life.

Elizabeth's process occupied a nine-month period. During this time she formed twelve sand pictures, not all of which I can present here. During the intervening hours we discussed her earlier pictures, her current dreams, and her intensive psychic engagement with the entire process. At the end we meticulously reviewed all the sand pictures in order to more firmly establish the transformation of her newly gained personality.

Elizabeth's transformation in such a relatively short time was made possible because she could accept the individual figures—selected at first more or less unconsciously—as partial aspects of herself. She did not attempt to shirk her responsibility toward these figures by projecting them onto her immediate environment. Through intensive dialogue and encounters with the individual sandplay figures, Elizabeth achieved consciousness concerning the powers active in her. We can therefore think of Elizabeth's sandplay process as being similar to a process of active imagination. This latter method is often recommended in Jungian psychology (see the glossary below).

In Illustration 40 I have assembled the most important figures which Elizabeth used frequently during sandplay. I have grouped them together here so that the reader can see each figure in greater detail.

Illustration 40

Elizabeth, the chief figures

Elizabeth's First Sand Picture

The overall impression of this picture is one of order and clarity. The semi-moist sand which forms the foundation is worked very little;

only a moat separates the upper right corner from the rest of the picture and a circle encloses a black spider. The main emphasis lies in the miniatures. We can see trees and houses, but few animals and ordinary people. The various groupings represent understandable scenes from daily life. This is the reason why I consider the picture to be relatively close to everyday consciousness. The two eye-catching central motifs are the encircled, black spider and the mother and child who are about to cross the bridge to go to another place. The main movement in the picture proceeds from the lower left toward the upper right, which, viewed schematically suggests that we are witnessing a development from a state of natural unconsciousness toward a more civilized consciousness. Elizabeth identified with the mother figure and during the hour expressed her feeling that her inner guiding image as a woman is undergoing a process of change. She was at a point of transition.

Let us first view the world from which the mother figure emerges. In the lower half of the picture toward the left we notice a small village. There, cheerful women dance, a country girl feeds the chickens, and a man and woman sit together at a dining table. Surely, this part of the picture expresses Elizabeth's contented family life in a country or village environment. The dancing women and the mother as well, move toward the bridge. Elizabeth is inwardly moved; she is looking forward to crossing over into another world.

In the upper left corner we notice a tree in bloom. In front of the tree stands a woman in a self-confident and upright posture who carries water, and next to her an old woman. Both of them seem to

Illustration 41

stand there in anticipation of the action, waiting to be ready to enter into it. The tree in bloom tells us that the two women underneath share in flourishing, spring-like hopes. In fact, it was spring when Elizabeth modelled this picture and she did have hopes that her life would change and she would 'blossom'. What all the figures meant, however, had not yet become clear to her. Elizabeth had chosen the woman carrying water because the upright posture intrigued her and because that woman was in possession, as she put it, of the water of life. Later Elizabeth mentioned that this figure represented to her the epitome of the independent, self-confident woman. This side was never developed in her. It hadn't had a chance. Moreover, she herself had often pushed back this side because of her belief that surely, a self-confident woman must be using energies egotistically, that is, only for herself, whereas a good mother should use all her available energies in the service of her husband and children.

Interestingly, it is the old woman who leads the water-carrying woman onto the stage of Elizabeth's 'world picture'. This old woman, Elizabeth noted later, represented the ancient, inner knowledge of a woman which could lead to development and wholeness. For Elizabeth she represented the awareness that the life of a woman is not exhausted by being a good wife and mother but could expand to include other areas of the personality, as for example the development of a more individual and intellectual point of view. Elizabeth mentioned later that this was the perfect time for the inner figure of the old wise woman to introduce to her the self-confidence needed to pass her examinations successfully.

Let us leave these two figures now because at this point they are merely standing there waiting. At the present time we only know, because of their position in the upper left corner, that they will play a role in Elizabeth's intellectual development.

Elizabeth said that in order to protect the other figures she isolated the black spider by enclosing it in a circle, because it might poison them. The black spider symbolized for her the shadowy sides of the good mother, especially her negative side which works to prevent the progress and development of her child. This can happen because of egotism or unconsciousness or, most dangerously, because the mother by virtue of her well-meaning care stifles and imprisons the child. Elizabeth also saw in the spider a quite influential person from her social circle who while pretending to be well-meaning always insinuated that Elizabeth would never pass her examinations nor complete her course of studies. On the other hand, Elizabeth also located in the spider her own fear of her studies and her inferiority complex which constantly suggested to her: 'Why do you need to study? Why do you need a new career? Don't you have a husband who cares for you (but who also tells you how you should see the world!)? And what about your dear children who are in such great need of you? Be satisfied with what you have!' When the inferiority complex speaks in this manner it can be very dangerous because there is always a grain of truth in such assertions. In general, these suggestions are devilish because the truth is twisted, and 'well-intended', 'loving' arguments are used to cover over one's own fear and inertia.

We all know this suggestive voice. Perhaps it sounds like this: 'Oh, Elizabeth, don't take on the time-consuming stress of graduate work; isn't it much better if both your husband and children can count on a well-rested wife and mother?' The 'devilish' aspect in such insinuations lies precisely in the fact that a mere housewife and mother doesn't rest at all because she always needs to justify her being 'merely' a mother and wife with yet more care and yet more service.

Nevertheless, we will see that the devilish spider that represents the shadowy sides of the 'good' mother also holds other aspects of the feminine imprisoned and these will become most valuable later on. But in this picture, as a precaution, the spider needed to be enclosed in a circle. The circle, however, highlights the spider, making it clear that the tension between the 'good mother' and the spider, in other words, her shadowy side, represents the central problem.

Let us also look at the upper right corner. For Elizabeth, this concentration of people and houses signified Paris as the city of world culture. Let us note that among other figures we can identify a nun and a pastor as representatives of religious life and a gypsy woman (with a yellow kerchief) and a very beautiful woman (with a white kerchief). In one form or another all of these figures will appear again later.

The motif of the city of Paris appeared in this sand picture because in real life Elizabeth was about to travel there. She was eagerly anticipating this trip because it would be the first time that she would venture forth from the family circle and travel as a free and independent woman. She expected to be greatly enriched by the cultural and artistic treasures of that city.

We can interpret this picture as follows: Elizabeth is at the beginning of a transition, an inner journey. Her ego is still mostly identified with the role of the good mother. As long as Elizabeth is dominated by this positive aspect of the mother archetype, her life is primarily spent loving and caring for her children and her husband. The shadowy side of the good mother, the negative aspect of the mother archetype, is consciously split off and simultaneously emphasized in the form of the black spider. In the following pictures we are well advised to watch for the particular aspects contained in this shadow.

The figure of the water-carrying woman as an image of the independent, self-confident woman belongs to another archetypal circle of the feminine. She stands ready in the upper left corner, from where, in my experience, important spiritual impulses appear, and looks toward the center. We may assume then that this water-carrying woman will become, guided by the old, wise woman, the central guiding image of Elizabeth's spiritual development.

The next picture (not shown here) was modelled after Elizabeth's return from Paris. I will describe two elements from it which are important for an understanding of the following pictures:

The woman carrying water was given a companion, the beautiful woman in a light blue dress. She carries a bouquet of flowers and in addition Elizabeth gave her a book, as a symbol of knowledge. Elizabeth intended that she represent that side of a woman which so often atrophies within traditional marriage and motherhood, namely the erotically and intellectually active side of a woman. This beautiful and dignified woman also shows us that Elizabeth did not equate an erotic woman with a 'loose' or suggestive woman. This was not her concern. Rather, she exemplified a fundamental openness for human and spiritual encounters outside the often constricting family circle.

Many women believe that faithfulness to their husbands includes sharing their husband's views and ideas. Such a view radically constricts the potential horizon of the woman and such a levelling of thoughts and life habits precludes any stimulation and renewal within the relationship of the couple. Eros really does mean something fundamentally different. Eros, as the God of love, is usually depicted as carrying a bow and arrow. It is rumored that no one is safe from his arrows. He wishes to strike all persons with his arrows, to awaken them. He wishes to connect people, to create encounters and relationships, to kindle love so that people will turn toward each other and prosper through mutual exchange and renewal. Every real encounter between two people, or between one person and another's creative work, and every encounter with nature signifies the crossing of the border of one's personal and narrow limits. It is always a challenge and an opportunity to extend one's own horizon. To encounter the wholly unknown, the wholly 'other', always brings a deeply numinous experience. Such encounters may lead to an experience of the divine and renew the person from top to bottom. This is why the appearance of this 'beautiful and erotic woman' carried great meaning for Elizabeth. By experiencing this side in herself she opened herself to the possibility of leaving behind her feelings of withdrawal and inferiority. She prepared herself to meet the 'other'. Knowledge was obviously part of this 'other', since the woman holds a book. We can see that the erotic-spiritual side of the feminine also belongs to the complex of the newly arising archetype.

The second small scene in this picture showed a loving, innocent country girl who is attacked by men on horseback, one of whom is a knight with a closed visor. Elizabeth became very much preoccupied with that scene. She asked herself the following: which aggressive, warlike side that does not show its face attacks this good, simple girl? I suggested to her to try to imagine the knight and open his visor so that she might recognize his face. Elizabeth did just this and at the next hour gained the following insight: the knight's face was her own angry face. It was her own expression of rage and aggression directed against her naive, girlish attitude which did not care to see what was hidden in the shadow of the good, loving mother. This rage was duly mixed with a great deal of frustration. After all, it was frustrating to learn for just how long she had repressed her personal and spiritual development and had used her energy in such great measure for her family. Did her family even need her concern to such a degree in order to prosper? Might her excessive mothering and protection even be harmful?

I pointed out that this anger which arises from within can be very healthy. The men on horseback and the knight represent a dynamic fighting energy which might serve her well once she learned to direct it not against herself but rather to use it, in the form of decisiveness and assertiveness, in the looming encounter with the spider.

I would like to mention here that it is much wiser to employ Eros, the beautiful woman, in the form of empathy in the encounter with the negative side of the mother archetype. Power begets power. If one uses empathy instead of power then one does not call up the opposing power of the negative mother which is overwhelming and destructive.

Elizabeth's Second Sand Picture

The dominant movement in this sand picture leads from the left toward the right, that is from the figure of the spinning woman at the left edge to the crucifix at the right edge. Such motion from left to right implies generally that we are witnessing both an emerging consciousness and a positive development toward the outer world. The mother and the woman carrying the water walk this way together. On the way, they encounter the kneeling woman whom

Illustration 42

Elizabeth called 'the meek one'. Just below this humble woman we can see the gypsy woman. In the first picture she was standing in the center of the city of Paris. Here she has possession of the book, the symbol of knowledge.

Let us first consider the spinning woman: This figure often appears in the sandplay processes of women during decisive moments of becoming conscious. The spinning woman is an ancient symbol for the working woman, or to be more exact, for the woman who can spin a thread from a natural product which will be used for weaving. The cloth is not a natural product but a work of culture. The spinning woman, therefore, is a primordial form of the feminine artisan creating culture. If she appears during sandplay, this indicates that a process of becoming conscious has been initiated.

We often say that the spinning woman spins our life thread and weaves our fate. Nordic mythology, for example, mentions the three strong female figures, the Norns, who spin the thread of fate:

> In the earliest period during the golden age the gods knew nothing of the Norns. They lived in blessed innocence and did not think of the passing of all things and the power of fate. But when they sullied themselves with sin, from the land of the giants three powerful sisters appeared. Their names are Urd, the Mistress of that which is past; Werdandi, who knows what is present and still becoming; and Skuld, who knows the future. Thus was ended the time of ignorance. From the giants, these three women have learned the fates of all the gods and humans.[54]

With the appearance of the spinning goddesses of fate, ignorance and blessed innocence is over. Knowledge of past, present and future, the flow of time and the mortality of mankind, and death enters consciousness. We know from Elizabeth's previous picture that for her the time of being an innocent, naive girl was over. It should not surprise us that it is quite possible even for a married woman and mother to still live out the innocent and unconscious attitude of a girl. But for Elizabeth the time had come to confront the question as to the meaning of her life. For her, this question was intimately tied to the question concerning her image of god. This is the reason why the acting figures in her sand picture are spread out between the spinning woman and the crucified Christ.

Our Christian image of Christ, the crucified son of God, is a picture of the suffering God. During sandplay children rarely use the crucified Christ to represent their image of God. Far more likely is that they use a Buddha image, or the baby Jesus, or an angel. They avoid the suffering or dead God. But for Elizabeth it was precisely the suffering aspect of the crucified Christ which carried great meaning. She saw the crucified 'meek one' and the gypsy woman as being connected with the black spider. How then are we to understand their relationship?

Elizabeth's look behind the visor of the knight had freed a great deal of energy in the form of rage and frustration. This energy aided Elizabeth in confronting the problem of the spider. Half consciously and half unconsciously, she pondered over this entire complex, until she finally realized that behind the spider there appeared her god-image, that is, her religious upbringing, which until then she had never really questioned.

Elizabeth explained the following: Basically, her upbringing had occurred within a tradition of the Christian religion which relegates women to a fundamentally serving, helping role. Women could enter careers as nurses, secretaries, and kindergarten teachers. Such professions were 'fitting' for a woman, but the highest profession suitable for a woman was to be an elementary school teacher. Being a wife and mother required that she serve, help, be kind and always available. If ever she deviated from this role, she would be accused of being evil, egotistical and unwomanly. In order to satisfy this collective image of the woman, she had assumed the attitude of the 'meek one'.

We might do well to scrutinize this kneeling figure which Elizabeth used during sandplay. She genuflects in the humblest of attitudes on the floor, has her hands folded as if she were praying or begging for something. Her hair, the personal honor and pride of a woman, is hidden under a bonnet, her head and eyes are cast downward. All she can possibly see is the little speck of earth in front of her knees! For centuries, freely flowing long hair had been the sign of the unmarried, free girl. The bonnet became the sign of the married woman and, at the same time, a symbol of the dependence and servitude within the marriage relationship.[55] Next to her is a loaf of bread and a basket filled with fruit.

For Elizabeth, the loaf of bread and the basket of fruit near the 'meek one' represented the wife's duty always to give and always to help and to care for her fellow human beings. She also mentioned that both the Church and many men (and women!) tried to keep women in this role. For them, it is indeed quite appealing and pleasant to have an ever-present, compassionate mother available. And at the same time, how convenient to know that a woman's humbly lowered eyes prevent her from seeing more of the world than was desired. Moreover, wasn't the suffering Christ, as our guiding image, designed to suggest that suffering belongs to the human condition? We do not have the right to revolt against this condition.

Many readers might now object and claim that such a wrongly understood role of the woman has long been outdated. It certainly ought to be this way, since so much has been written and spoken about this topic. But in everyday reality the picture is different. Quite a few women and men hold fast to the notion, perhaps not in their heads but nonetheless in their hearts, that a real woman and especially a good mother should always be available, sacrificing, and loving. It is obvious that such expectations are inhuman, yet they are often the order of the day.

To accuse someone of egotism is not as grave an accusation as it once was. But to accuse a woman of being unwomanly or worse still, being evil, when in reality, she only tries to raise her head high and to acknowledge that besides being a mother she has other needs, wounds most women deeply. Elizabeth too had been hurt, although in her case, her self-accusations were more destructive than those coming from others.

To confront the negative forces within oneself is a most difficult challenge and it requires a great deal of honesty, courage, and differentiation. It is not simply a question of eliminating them out of hand. Entrenched patterns of behavior cannot be changed at a moment's notice. What is required, above all, is to recognize such patterns and become conscious of how they manifest themselves in daily life. Then, through careful self-observation one must avoid falling back into the old habits. After gaining insight into one's own nature, there comes the daily, laborious work on one's self, of living one's life in a new and conscious way. I do not believe in miracles that would instantly change the psychic structure of a human being.

For example, Elizabeth could now have renounced her role as housewife and mother, together with the attitudes in which she had been raised and which were grounded in a falsely understood humility. She did not want to do this, because her loving relationship to her husband and children filled an actual need in her. It was because of this that the figure of the woman who carries water had such great meaning for her and strengthened her positively experienced motherhood. After all, a woman can be a wife and mother and walk with her head proudly held high, knowing her self-worth. This is especially true if her personal work and interests are given both inner and outer recognition and keep her balanced!

Over a period of time, Elizabeth gained strength through yet another figure, that of the gypsy. In this sand picture it was she who possessed knowledge. Many of the feminine qualities modern women like to project onto gypsy women (the gypsy woman appears often in sandplay therapies), have long ago been repressed into the unconscious because of the one-sided preference for a false feminine humility. There, in the shadow, they live an atrophied existence. This can clearly be seen in these sand pictures as well. The spider, which personified the shadow of the perennial good mother, released its contents only after Elizabeth demonstrated her decisiveness. And what came to light was the figure of the negative, 'meek one', as well as the figure of the knowing, and therefore positive, gypsy woman.

The essence of the gypsy woman is closely connected to the nature of the witch. Today, in innumerable books, the latter enjoys an enormous revival. Both gypsy women and witches, even for a rationally thinking person, are dark, uncanny, and yet fascinating. The knowledge of the gypsy or witch, which includes both the knowledge of the healing and toxic powers of nature, and the secrets surrounding life and death or of the great, invisible powers of human beings, has been lost to most modern women. Yet this great ancient knowledge is present in the unconscious and preoccupies mankind, male and female. It is well known that once there existed white and black witches, and that there is white and black magic, powers which may be used for good or evil. For this reason it is important that they are not projected onto witches and gypsies. Rather, such powers are to be recognized and made conscious within us in order that we may learn to act responsibly with them. As I have mentioned already in the introduction, in order to harness such powers, it is of utmost importance that we refine our senses and intuition, that we learn to differentiate and pay conscious attention to the world of our instincts and body consciousness as well as the products of the imaginal world, and gain knowledge through the careful observation of both inner and outer nature.

While Elizabeth possessed many of these skills already, they nonetheless needed to be redeemed from their shadowy existence within her and assigned their proper place in her life. Once Elizabeth had integrated the energies released by the gypsy woman she experienced a further strengthening of her personality.

Before we go on to the next picture, let us attend to the round, red apple in the left corner. We often find in either the upper or lower left hand corner single symbols which foreshadow a coming development. They are precursors of thematic configurations being constellated in the unconscious which will appear in a more elaborate form in the sand only after some time has elapsed.

Elizabeth's Third Sand Picture

Illustration 43

This sand picture is especially beautiful and radiates great strength. The four corners are emphasized with strong trees in bloom. In the central, circular hollow lie five shiny, red apples. Surrounding these are all of the feminine figures we have come to know so far. There are some male figures present as well. All the figures appear connected, united, and they concentrate on the red apples in the center.

To the left of the circle stands the spinning woman. We could ask if it was she who achieved the union of all these forces?

If we look at the male figures we find a light-bearer, a flute player, a shepherd, and a dancing young man. There is no ruling figure or warrior in the entire circle. From the point of view of analytical psychology and using its language, we would say that these masculine figures represent Elizabeth's masculine side, her animus.

Here, he shows himself in very positive guises, representing enlight-
enment, movement, and enthusiasm. In fact, all figures radiate
peace, joy, strength, and life. And the five apples in the middle are
similarly healthy and lively. Red or golden apples have always been
symbols of fertility and love. If we give another person a shiny red
apple there is always a sense of congeniality or a touch of the erotic
associated with the act which says: 'I like you!' It has been my
experience that red apples are predominantly used by women who
feel happy and fruitful. They all blossom through their relationships
and their capacity for love. The fact that there are five apples is also
significant. The number five and the pentagram—the five-pointed
star-shaped figure—are ancient symbols of the great goddesses of
love: Isis, Ishtar, Aphrodite, and Venus (The pentagram is related to
the orbit of the planet Venus).[56] Thus, the number five adds to the
erotic symbolism of the apples. But even if we knew nothing
concerning such symbolism, the apples would still appeal to us
because of their red color and form. They represent vitality, love,
sexuality, dynamism, sensuality, and joy. Elizabeth did not know
very much about the symbolism of the individual figures. For her the
picture represented the moment when all her energies began to serve
Eros and could be used in the service of love and committed
relationship.

Elizabeth's Fourth Sand Picture

Illustration 44

Here we find the motif of the apples again, surrounded by four people. This picture seems like a miniature of the great archetypal motif which appeared in the previous sand picture. If we look at the fine lines which are formed in the surface of the sand we can recognize the schematic outlines of a human being with arms and legs spread apart. In the upper center we can see a rounded elevation which could suggest the head. Looked at in this way, the four persons surrounding the apples are located in the place of the heart and all other figures are oriented in their direction.

Elizabeth had formed this sand picture unconsciously. When at the end of the hour I pointed out to her the human body in the sand and that all energies seemed to point to the location of the heart, she replied, "Yes, I do feel a new strength and confidence within myself."

I interpreted this picture as follows: The previous sand picture showed that in Elizabeth the great archetypal energy of connecting Eros had been constellated. The circle, oriented toward a central focus, manifests the ordering and centering energy of the Self which is always a moving and numinous experience. A sand picture of this kind has a long-lasting effect in the person who forms it. It becomes an inner source of peace and strength. This picture took hold of Elizabeth's heart. It gave her a feeling of wholeness and strength. This enabled her to overcome her initial inner discord, and she began to look forward to her examinations with confidence.

The four figures surrounding the apples are meaningful also in themselves. We see the beautiful woman, the flute player, the wise old woman and a wise old man. This quaternity unites the opposites of male and female, and young and old. It is a symbol of wholeness. The flute player by virtue of his music adds a very special vibrant and lively mood to the scene because sound, music, establishes the connection between heaven and earth, and God and man.[57] This relationship between God and man is aroused through the vibrations of the heart, that is, feeling. Here, this subjective feeling is in the service of the ego and forms the connection to the Self. It acts much like a rod which steadies us and points us in the direction of the journey toward inner wholeness.

Elizabeth's Fifth Sand Picture

First, we might notice here the newly added element of water. A small tributary enters the picture from the lower edge of the tray. The figures are grouped in a large oval around two centers. The one to the right contains a tall, beautiful tree which Elizabeth called the tree of

Illustration 45

life; the one to the left, an elongated stone which she placed there as a manifestation or confirmation of her personality. Surrounding the stone are the woman who carries the water and the book, the wise old woman, a red apple, the old man, the lantern-carrier, and an empty bench. We might well wonder, why is this bench here? Is it for the beautiful woman or an 'unknown' figure, male or female? Next to the tree we see the flute player, the gypsy woman, a small white horse and the mother and all the way to the right, there is again the 'meek one'. This time she is accompanied by an interesting figure, a cock. Now, the cock usually, has a very special meaning: he crows at break of day. He greets the returning daylight, the brightness which makes all things visible and discernable. Perhaps he symbolizes the fact that the essence of the 'meek one' needs to be illuminated still further.

In this picture, it seemed to me, the creek and the small figure with the red skirt just above the water, is very important. Here we see a second figure, a woman who also carries water, only she is much smaller. She carries the water from the tributary to the other people.

Let us recall that for Elizabeth the first woman carrying water represented the epitome of the self-confident woman who also has the water of life. This great water-carrying woman is an archetypal figure, an impersonal guiding image in Elizabeth's psyche. The little woman, however, as she said herself, represents Elizabeth herself. Now she too has the water of life. This is living water. Flowing water is a symbol for the energy of life which is moved and moves us. The tributary is the unconscious from which new life energy can be drawn forever. Elizabeth has found the source of her life's energy within herself. We can now understand why the woman who carries the water is so self-confident. She can be self-confident because she has living water. She has become conscious of the power of her Self and draws from it her own life energy.

Elizabeth's Sixth Sand Picture

Illustration 46

We are aware now that Elizabeth can even call two sources of energy her own. One tributary comes from below, the realm of the earth or the material world to which the body belongs as well; the other originates from the upper edge, from the sky, the realm of the superior or archetypal forces. We could also say that one energy source comes from the earth, the realm of matter and the other from heaven, the realm of the spiritual. But we should avoid falling into the common dichotomy, the split between matter and spirit. Therefore, I prefer to speak of the spirit of the earth and the spirit of heaven approaching each other, seeking to find connection.

In the place where such a possible union might occur, both the woman carrying water and the 'meek one' face each other. Once again they seek an encounter. The other figures are placed discreetly somewhat in the background but look with concentrated attention at the meeting of the two. Let us note that next to the 'meek one' there is a donkey. I have discussed the symbolism of the donkey in detail earlier. In this sand picture the donkey is related to the meek side in Elizabeth's character, her long-suffering and forbearance of her shadow side. The donkey also represented the suffering over one's material nature and body, because after Elizabeth had done a great deal of thinking and feeling about this problem, she had come to the conclusion that the kneeling figure did not only represent the false humility; rather the figure also represented the very real suffering, her own suffering over her ignorance and unconsciousness. What was meant here is somewhat similar to Maria's insight that a person's unconsciousness can turn into suffering and become a source of great distress, but then again, this suffering may also set in motion a developmental process leading to consciousness. In this picture the suffering side of Elizabeth's personality, as it were, kneels down in her distress and asks Elizabeth's other side, represented by the woman carrying water, for help. After all, she knows the sources of knowledge and can make conscious that which is unconscious. Let us now ask how we can relate this interplay of the individual figures to Elizabeth's practical life.

First of all, Elizabeth had to recognize and take seriously her suffering over her inferiority complex and her far too narrow consciousness. Then she had to realize that her feelings of inferiority were not irreversible, either for religious or social reasons, or because she was a woman. In this respect the self-confident attitude of the woman carrying water, the beautiful woman and the gypsy, were very helpful. It goes without saying that I, of course, supported these figures, whenever they appeared in the sand, for they represented Elizabeth's inner attitudes.

It would not be unwarranted to imagine that Elizabeth's increasing self-confidence might have led her to develop delusions of grandeur. But there was never any danger of that! In general it might be said that there simply wasn't any time for such a thing. In other words, her ongoing course of studies, in addition to the preparations necessary to take her examination, while at the same time still caring for a family, prevented her fantasies from getting out of hand. For Elizabeth to accomplish all of her many tasks successfully it required willpower, perseverance, and especially individual ability. I mentioned earlier that from a sunflower there will never come a rose and from a small violet never a great, strong oak tree. Elizabeth's insight into her own strengths and limitations found expression in the next picture where we meet a new figure.

Elizabeth's Seventh Sand Picture

The two tributaries have become one and form a single, round lake which lies there as if it were an opening to that other reality, the reality of the psyche. Let us recall that the watery world representing

Illustration 47

the world of the flowing and moving psychic energy, forms the connection between the world of the absolute, the archetypal world, and the material world. In this realm between spirit and matter lies the psychic world of the imagination, or in terms of analytical psychology, the realm of the archetypal images. These inner images are enriched by psychic energy and can become a source of strength for the person.

In this sand picture nine figures forming a circle stand around the water. There are fewer figures here than in the third sand picture (Illustration 43); nonetheless each figure had special significance for Elizabeth. The many figures in the third sand picture symbolized a great quantity of energy, whereas here, fewer figures represent a more differentiated, meaningful quality.

The wise old couple embody the ancient wisdom which speaks to us from the unconscious during very special and important moments; the woman carrying water along with the two light-bearers stand for Elizabeth's bright, clear, and self-confident side; the dancing couple represented, as she said, the union—through feeling—of her masculine and feminine sides, and the gypsy woman embodied forces in Elizabeth which are closer to nature; the darker powers coming from the unconscious. Finally, at the right side and enclosed in the circle, we can see the simple, kneeling African figure made of wood. After considering the meaning of this figure for quite some time, Elizabeth accepted it as representation both of a genuine humility toward existence and of a genuine feminine devotion to life. For Elizabeth this meant an acceptance of her own fate, but this acceptance was not engendered through her acquired inferiority complex, but rather by objectively estimating her own abilities. She also connected with this figure her insight, acquired through experience, that the unconscious psyche knows infinitely more than the conscious mind and evolves in unpredictable ways not readily comprehensible. It seems to me that an invisible thread connects this internalized kneeling figure with the spinning woman.

The closed circle of figures which surrounds the circular lake represents Elizabeth's psychic wholeness as it existed at this time. This wholeness seems to have emerged from the figure of the mother who stands next to the circle. We can see that Elizabeth's motherliness was neither lost nor repressed but has changed into a much more comprehensive and differentiated womanhood. I have not been able to find a readily available mythological image in which motherhood, eros, and spirituality are contained, one which could serve as a comprehensive, feminine guiding image and which would be inclusive of a professional career. It seems to me that we are confronted in this century with this newly forming archetype of the modern woman.

Elizabeth's understanding of herself as a woman changed from an earlier form into another, new form. In contrast to a healing process, I prefer to call it a process of transformation.

A further reflection is needed concerning the mother figure which now stands outside the circle. It seems to me that this figure does not just represent Elizabeth's own motherliness. The figure stands next to the strong tree of life and the flourishing, little village so that we, I believe, are entitled to view the entire group as carrying one meaning. Together, it may represent Elizabeth's healthy and prospering start in life, her happily experienced mother-child relationship. In this primal relationship with her mother she had been able to form a secure attachment. That is the reason why the figure of the mother, representing the fountain of strength, accompanied Elizabeth during the entire process of transformation.

If we recall the suffering and difficulties which Eva had to face before she could accept her life, who had first to learn how to live, then we can fathom in some measure what valuable potential Elizabeth brought into our therapeutic situation in the first place. Because of such a good starting foundation and because she expended tremendous effort in completing both her course of studies and in participating in her analytic 'work', Elizabeth was able to overcome the early injury to her feelings of self-confidence which she suffered when she entered school and was judged to be a retarded child. A person can become educated and gain self-awareness through his own inner and outer work. Just as the spinning woman does, any person can take an active part in spinning the thread of his or her own psychological development and humanization.

To me it seems important to note that an intensive inner and outer effort can not only overcome feelings of inferiority in spiritual and intellectual areas, but also compensate for the support which a father might have provided in these domains. It is the father's task to strengthen and guide the child in the confrontation with the masculine values dominating the world of work and intellect. If the father was absent or neglected this, the analyst can temporarily fill this role and function.

The confrontation and integration of such masculine values does not necessarily imply that the woman must become masculine or turn into a so-called bluestocking. In Elizabeth's pictures we continuously come across the dancing couple representing the joyful feelings of the union of her masculine and feminine sides. Elizabeth could assume such a vibrant and erotically informed attitude toward the masculine the moment her own feminine feelings of self-confidence and self-assertion began to blossom. Would we be wrong to assume that it was the beautiful, red apple in the second sand picture (Illustration 42) which initiated that vibrant feeling of union between the dancing couple?

Finally, I would like to draw attention to the little rider on a white horse who enters the last sand picture from the lower left corner. He is lying down—by mistake; originally he was meant to ride toward the center. It is fair to assume that this little man on horseback stands for Elizabeth herself. It is also quite correct to assume that Elizabeth's process of self-realization is not ended just because of this picture. The white horse is the symbol for a bright, spiritual, and religious power[58] which will carry her further on her way.

The sandplay process which I have illustrated here ended after a nine-month period. Elizabeth continued her psychological work in a verbal analysis. She passed her examinations and finished her course of studies.

Once again I would like to emphasize that during these nine months Elizabeth intensively confronted herself, and me, as her analyst. Very little of this latter process can be shared with the reader. But the most important stations of Elizabeth's confrontation with the unconscious have truly been captured in the seven sand pictures which I have presented and discussed here.

Conclusion

The previous series of sand pictures has allowed us to cast a glance into the infinitely varied world of the psyche. Surely, we can never lay hold of this interstitial realm in its entirety, yet it is there where the spirit and body, the inner and the outer, the conscious and unconscious are woven together. Every person who makes sand pictures forms his worlds in the most personal of ways. Indeed, I have never seen two sand pictures which were alike, and yet sand pictures join the common and shared, archetypal patterns with individual development.

The precondition for the therapeutic method of sandplay, and incidentally for the verbal analytic method as well, is a knowledge of the individual and collective psyche, its structure and disturbances, its potential for healing and transformation. Both methods are rooted in the same depth-psychological training. The sandplay therapist, however, will need additional specific experience and training in the sandplay method.

During a verbal analysis, the analyst and analysand sit across from each other. In the classical Freudian setting, the analysand lies on the couch and the analyst sits behind him. Contrary to either of these methods, during sandplay the analysand is clearly in the center of the action. The heart of this action is clearly the holistic activity of the analysand. He is totally involved with his body, psyche, and spirit at the sand tray.

Sandplay heals not by being acted upon by another, but rather by the analysand's own action. Through the analysand's creations and attitude the energies at work within him are made externally visible. We can speak of each sand picture as being an actual act of birth. This is so because the analysand does indeed present that which is innermost to the outside. He cannot hide, he must take responsibility for that which he expresses. Obviously, this makes for a most intimate relationship between the analysand and the analyst which requires the utmost in trust and respect. Often a word spoken aloud may be incorrect since after a birth, such as the creative act, a person is quite vulnerable. Therefore, what is required of the analyst is restraint and a fine sensibility.

121

And yet creative expression is not associated only with vulnerability; there is also a great joy! In every sandplay therapy there comes a moment when the analysand looks proudly and happily upon his 'creation', often amazed at how fascinatingly different his newly created picture is, compared with those things in the world he had known previously. Joy in the face of creativity seems to be the attitude which we find repeatedly at the beginning of the healing process. I believe that this joyful acceptance of his own creation also marks the acceptance of his own creative potential, and most importantly himself.

Sandplay activates the deepest layers of the unconscious and, as we have seen in the case of Eva, months and years may go by until the developments foreshadowed in the sand pictures can be realized in conscious life. Yet this inherent diagnostic potential is extraordinarily valuable to the analyst. It helps him to have patience and confidence in the directions and goals of the inner process in the analysand, and to support it even when the analysand becomes impatient and demands immediate and visible changes in his life. All true transformations in a person take much time. It is possible, however, for the analysand to experience immediately at the sand tray the liberating effect and joy contained within his own creative actions.

Glossary

Active Imagination

Active imagination is different from passive imagination in that the person's conscious ego enters into an active confrontation with the imaginal figures arising from the unconscious. What follows is a dialogue or confrontation between the conscious ego and the more or less unconscious, inner figures. On the one hand, such a process may be difficult to bear and on the other it includes the possibility of a very intensive encounter with the unconscious and the possibility of a vast widening of consciousness. The method of active imagination requires a solidly grounded ego.

On active imagination, see also: Hannah, Barbara. *Encounters with the Soul: Active Imagination as Developed by C.G. Jung.* Boston: Sigo Press, 1981, and Kast, Verena. *Imagination als Raum der Freiheit.* Olten/Freiburg i.Br.: Walter, 1988. Also Johnson, Robert. *Inner Work: Using Dreams and Active Imagination for Personal Growth.* New York: Harper and Row, 1986.

Amplification

Material associative and analogous to symbols and images from dreams and the imagination can provide clues for understanding symbols derived from the unconscious.

Archetype and Archetypal Image

When I speak of archetypes in this book, I mean the dynamic structural elements in the human psyche which seem, on the one hand, to be inborn, and on the other, acquired by life experience. They are responsible, among other things, for the origin of similar or analogous symbolic images among vastly differing peoples and cultures. The archetypes as such are non-representational and incapable of being made conscious; nonetheless their effect upon the human psyche can be seen in the inexhaustible variety of personal and collective archetypal images.

The archetypal image is the personal or collective image which may be formed under the influence of archetypal energy within an individual or a collective. Since psychic life is in continuous flux, archetypal images should not be conceived as unchanging forms. Rather, they change and develop in accordance with the transforma-

123

tion and development of the person. "Not for a moment dare we succumb to the illusion that an archetype can be finally explained and disposed of. Even the best attempts at explanation are only more or less successful translations into another metaphorical language." (Jung, C.G. CW, vol. 9, i, par. 271.)

Association Experiment
The association experiment is a method developed by depth psychology to test and determine the existence of complexes and extends our knowledge of associations. The test measures the reaction times, the verbal and nonverbal answers, and other reactions to given stimulus words.

Cerebral Hemispheres (Left and Right)
The left cerebral hemisphere governs the right side of the body and the right cerebral hemisphere the left side of the body. Typical characteristics and functions are:

Left Cerebral Hemisphere:	Right Cerebral Hemisphere:
Verbal	Nonverbal
Rational	Nonrational
Logical	Intuitive
Linear	Holistic
Analytical	Synthetic
Abstract	Concrete
Temporally consecutive	'Thinks' in images
Connected to consciousness	Reduced connection to consciousness
	The *corpus callosum* connects the right cerebral hemisphere to the left side.
	Dominant in the control of emotions

Extraversion
"Extraversion is an outward-turning of libido. . . . Everyone in the extraverted state thinks, feels, and acts in relation to the object. . . . Extraversion is a transfer of interest from subject to object. . . . Extraversion is active when it is intentional, and passive when the object compels it, i.e., when the object attracts the subject's interest of its own accord, even against his will. When extraversion is habitual, we speak of the extraverted type." (Jung, C.G. CW, vol. 6, par. 710.)

Individuation

"Individuation is the central concept of Jungian (Analytical) psychology. In general, it is the process by which individual beings become themselves, that is, the process by which an individual realizes much of the potential within his personality. Individuation is not to be confused with mere egoistic self-realization. On the contrary, individuation unites the person with his own depths and causes him to take his connectedness to existing social and cultural factors seriously. The process of individuation at the same time leads the individual to greater consciousness of himself, as well as the world at large, and fosters an awareness of the inherent reciprocity of the individual and the world.

"C.G. Jung conceived of life as a process which continuously demands that the person mature or adapt in incremental steps. Jung conceptualized the human psyche according to the various aspects he chose to investigate. From this view the individual is always more than his conscious ego. To become conscious of the unconscious parts of one's psyche and to work toward their integration is the task demanded by individuation. The individual, therefore, remains open to life as a process of becoming till the end, that is, until the final goal of his life is reached." (Asper, Kathrin. *Verlassenheit und Selbstentfremdung.* Olten/Freiburg i.Br.: Walter, 1987)

Inflation

When an individual identifies with a greater personality (ideal) or with an archetype, it may cause him to become inflated. Such a person has extended himself beyond his own individual proportions and limitations. The resulting puffed-up condition does not correspond to reality.

Introversion

"Introversion means an inward-turning of libido. . . . Interest does not move towards the object but withdraws from it into the subject. Everyone whose attitude is introverted thinks, feels, and acts in a way that clearly demonstrates that the subject is the prime motivating factor and that the object is of secondary importance. Introversion . . . is active when the subject voluntarily shuts himself off from the object, passive when he is unable to restore to the object the libido streaming back from it. When introversion is habitual, we speak of an introverted type." (Jung, C.G. CW, vol. 6, par. 770.)

Progression and Regression of Psychic Energy

A progression implies the forward movement of psychic energy which leads the individual to adapt continually to the conditions of the external world. A regression implies the retrograde and inward movement of psychic energy which adapts the individual to the conditions of his inner world. During a regression, contents of the unconscious are activated or reactivated which had been 'slumbering' there, or which developmentally and temporally are located far in the past of the individual, or which had been repressed. During the following progression of energy such contents may lead the way toward development. In principle, however, both progression and regression of psychic energy must be viewed as a reciprocal animation of the external and internal world and should not be confused with either developmental progress or regression.

Projection
"Projection . . . is an unconscious, automatic process whereby a content that is unconscious to the subject transfers itself to an object, so that it seems to belong to that object. The projection ceases the moment it becomes conscious, that is to say when it is seen as belonging to the subject." (Jung, C.G. CW, vol. 9, i, par. 121; see also von Franz, M.-L. *Projection and Re-Collection in Jungian Psychology: Reflections of the Soul.* La Salle: Open Court, 1985, pp. 1ff.)

Quaternity
A quaternity corresponds to the principle of order and wholeness. We speak of the four directions in order to describe the totality of the horizon or in order to be able to orient ourselves. A totality is also expressed, for example, by the four elements, the four seasons, and in analytical psychology by the four psychological functions: sensation, thinking, feeling, and intuition.

Rites of Passage
Passage from one period of the life cycle to another is accompanied by changes which are more or less difficult to accomplish. Rites of passage may aid, assist, and help order such periods of transition. The most important transitions are birth, marriage, death, and the various initiations, such as passing into another age level, another career or social group. In therapeutic work with children and teenagers the initiation rites which regulate the transition from childhood to adulthood are especially important.

The structure of rites of passage is always the same: after the rites of separation which dissolve the ties of the individual to the previous period in the life cycle there follows a more or less lengthy period of transition. During this time the individual is extremely vulnerable because he is 'uncontained'. Through rites of initiation the individual is then integrated into a new period of his life. This entrance is always connected with the person assuming a new social role.

Self

In analytical psychology the Self represents the central archetype of unity and totality of the whole person to which the ego is subordinated. Therefore, the Self comprises conscious and unconscious, experiential and non-experiential, or those things not yet made available to experience. The Self is the archetype of order, and the effect of this ordering principle can in turn be experienced by the psyche.

"The Self represents the psycho-biological totality which influences development throughout the life cycles. Simultaneously, it is the goal of the process of individuation insofar as the individual devotes himself to developmental impulses rather than to closing himself off from developing toward wholeness. Essential to such wholeness is the religious dimension. Jung understood the Self as a god image within the psyche as well as the psychic organ capable of perceiving that which is divine and eternal." (Asper, Kathrin. *Verlassenheit and Selbstentfremdung*. Olten/Freiburg i.Br.: Walter, 1987, p. 17)

Empirically the Self can be made visible in many ways, including multi-dimensional forms and designs, in dreams, myths, and fairy tales as the 'supra-ordinate personality'; for example as king or queen, hero or heroine, as savior, or as circle, square, mandala, cross, or the Tao, or again as the focus of the interplay between the opposites of yin and yang.

Shadow

The shadow in analytical psychology signifies those parts of a person's personal and collective psyche which cannot be lived out in reality because of their incompatibility with his consciously chosen values and forms of life. Such parts are usually the darker, repressed, or undeveloped aspects of the personality. The shadow, however, may contain both negative and positive elements.

Symbol

The symbol unites the tangible world of objects with the psychic and spiritual world. The objects contained in our environment, our actions, and the world of appearances contain yet another dimension of meaning over and above their immediately apparent purpose. The meaning of this spiritual dimension may be more or less conscious to us, but the symbol always unites the material with the spiritual, the conscious with the unconscious aspects of an object of appearance into a totality.

"A symbol always presupposes that the chosen expression is the best possible description or formulation of a relatively unknown fact, which is nonetheless known to exist or is postulated as existing." (Jung, C.G. CW, vol. 6, par. 814)

Transference and Countertransference
The phenomenon of transference occurs when during the course of treatment the analysand experiences the analyst as the bad or perennial 'good' and loving mother, as the stern father, as an omniscient demigod, etc. The analyst too can make analogous mistakes about his analysand in both a positive and negative sense: this latter phenomenon is known as countertransference. What one strives for during the course of analysis then, is the transformation of such transference and countertransference into more of a reality-connected and mutual relationship which includes both one's own and the other person's possibilities and limitations. (For transference and countertransference see: Jacoby, M. *Psychotherapeuten sind auch Menschen*. Olten/Freiburg i.Br.: Walter, 1987)

Notes

Preface

1. Harding, Gosta. *Spieldiagnostiik*. Basel/Weinheim: Beltz, 1972.
2. Kalff, Dora M. *Sandplay*. Boston: Sigo Press, 1980.
3. Jung, C.G. *Memories, Dreams, Reflections*. New York: Random House, 1965, pp. 173ff.
4. For disturbances of early childhood and narcissistic disturbances, see Asper, Kathrin. *Verlassenheit und Selbstentfremdung*. Olten/Freiburg i.Br.: Walter, 1987.

Chapter 1

5. See: Ammann, Ruth. *Eine Kinderanalyse anhand von Sandbildern*. Diplomate Thesis, C.G. Jung-Institut, Zurich, 1979.
6. Weinrib, Estelle. *Images of the Self*. Boston: Sigo Press, 1983.
7. Asper, Kathrin. *Verlassenheit und Selbstentfremdung*. *Op.cit*. See especially the chapter 'Therapeutische Haltung' (The Therapeutic Attitude).
8. Eccles, John E. *The Understanding of the Brain*. New York: McGraw-Hill, 1973.
9. Achterberg, Jeanne. *Imagery in Healing: Shamanism and Modern Medicine*. Boston: New Science Library, 1985. Especially the chapter 'Science and the Imagination: Physiology and Biochemistry'.
10. Ammann, Ruth. *Traumbild Haus*. Olten/Freiburg i. Br.: Walter, 1987. Especially chapter 1: 'Die Wechselwirkung zwischen Mensch und Haus' (The Reciprocal Influence between the Person and his House).
11. van der Post, Laurens. 'Die Wildnis im Garten der Seele', in *Spinx-Magazin*, H. 32 Juni/Juli 1985.
12. Jung, C.G. *Memories, Dreams, and Reflections*. New York: Random House, 1965, pp. 200ff.
13. Jung, C.G. *Collected Works* [abbr. CW], 2d ed. Princeton: Princeton University Press, 1970, vol. 14, par. 447.
14. CW, vol. 12, par. 401 and 403.

Chapter 2

15. Ammann, Ruth. *Traumbild Haus. Op.cit.* Especially Chapter 4: 'Lebensräume—Lebensträume' (Life spaces—Life dreams).
16. Kalff, Dora M. *Sandplay. Op.cit.* p. 30.

Chapter 3

17. CW, vol. 8, par. 158, 135, 159.
18. CW, vol. 9, i, par. 289.
19. CW, vol. 6, par. 758.

Chapter 4

20. CW, vol. 12, par. 394.
21. Markale, Jean. *Die Druiden.* München: Dianus-Trikont, 1985. Especially chapter 4: 'Die geistige Welt der Druiden' (The spiritual world of the Druids).
22. Capra, Fritjof. *The Turning Point: Science, Society and the Rising Culture.* New York: Simon and Schuster, 1982.
23. von Franz, M.-L. *Projection and Re-Collection in Jungian Psychology: Reflections of the Soul.* La Salle, Ill.: Open Court, 1980.
24. Bischof, Marco. *Unsere Seele kann fliegen.* Especially the chapter: 'Druiden, keltisches Christentum und Geomantie' (Druids, Celtic Christianity and Geomancy). Frauenfeld: Verlag im Waldgut, 1985.
25. Achterberg, Jeanne. *Imagery in Healing: Shamanism and Modern Medicine.* Especially the chapter 'Science and the Imagination: Physiology and Biochemistry', *Op.cit.* pp. 113–141.

Chapter 6

26. CW, vol. 6, pars. 789–791.
27. CW, vol. 9, pars. 627ff. and 713ff.
28. Asper, Kathrin. *Verlassenheit und Selbstentfremdung. Op.cit.* p. 68.
29. Tansley, David V. *Energiekörper.* München: Kösel, 1985, p. 78.
30. CW, vol. 13, par. 134.
31. For 'snake' see CW, vol. 12, par. 184. For 'skull' or 'death's head' see CW, vol. 12, par. 107. For *mortificatio* and *nigredo* see CW, vol. 12, par. 334.
32. For 'dismemberment' see Eliade, Mircea. *Shamanism: Archaic Techniques of Ecstasy.* Translated by W.R. Trask. New York (Bollingen Series LXXVI) and London: 1964, p. 53ff.

33. CW, vol. 16, par. 475ff.
34. Duerr, Hans Peter. *Sedna*. Frankfurt/M.: Suhrkamp, 1984. Especially the chapter 'The Lady of the Labyrinth'. p. 142ff.
35. Riedel, Ingrid. *Traumbild Fuchs*. Olten/Freiburg i.Br.: Walter, 1978.
36. See Heinz-Mohr, Gerd. *Lexikon der Symbole*. München: Diederichs, 1983, p. 280.
37. For 'Khidr', see CW, vol. 5, pars. 282 and 285; also Jung's unpublished *Kindertraumseminar Winter 1940–41*. Zurich: Schippert, 1976, p. 57ff.
38. CW, vol. 9, i, par. 289.
39. For 'quaternity' see CW, vol. 12, par. 283.
40. Heinz-Mohr, Gerd. *Lexikon der Symbole. Op.cit.*, p. 311; and Götze, Heinz. *Castel del Monte*. München: Prestel, 1984.
41. CW, vol. 12, par. 334.

Chapter 7

42. For a detailed description of the analysis of a child and amplification of animal symbolism, see Ammann, Ruth: *Eine Kinderanalyse anhand von Sandbildern. Op.cit.*
43. Neumann, Erich. *The Child: Structure and Dynamics of the Nascent Personality*. New York: Putnam's Sons, 1973. Especially chapter 2.
44. Eliade, Mircea. *The Sacred and the Profane: The Nature of Religion*. New York: Harcourt, Brace and Company, 1959, pp. 34-36.
45. *Ibid.*, p. 184ff.
46. See 'donkey' in Collodi, Carlo. *Pinocchios Abenteuer*. Köln: Röderberg, 1983; and von Franz, M.-L. *The Golden Ass*. Zurich-New York: Spring Publications, 1990.
47. For 'mouse' see *Handwörterbuch des deutschen Aberglaubens*. Berlin 1927-1942, vol. 6.
48. Neumann, Erich. *The Child*. Especially the third chapter, *Op.cit.* p. 81.
49. For 'colors' see Itten, Johannes. *Kunst der Farbe*. Ravensburg: Ravensburger Buchverlag, 1970; and Riedel, Ingrid. *Farben*. Stuttgart: Kreuz, 1983.
50. CW, vol. 16, pars. 477, 478.
51. Neumann, Erich. *The Child*. Especially chapter 5: 'The Stages in the Child's Ego-Development', *Op.cit.* p. 136.
52. *Ibid.*
53. Eliade, Mircea. *Rites and Symbols of Initiation: The Mysteries of Birth and Rebirth*. New York: Harper & Row, 1965.

Chapter 8

54. Peterich, Eckart. *Götter und Helden der Germanen*. Olten/Freiburg
    i. Br.: Walter, 1937, p. 23; and *Die Edda*. Düsseldorf: Diederichs,
    1933, p. 44ff.
55. For 'bonnet' see *Handwörterbuch d. deutschen Aberglaubens. Op.cit.*
56. For 'Five' see Endres, F.C.: *Mystik und Magie der Zahlen*. Zurich/
    Stuttgart: Rascher, 1951.
57. Ammann, Peter. 'Musik und Seele'. Diplomate Thesis, C.G. Jung In-
    stitute, Zurich, 1965.
58. For 'horse', see *Handwörterbuch d. deutschen Aberglaubens. Op.cit.*

Index

Printed in the United States
3449